Monetary Policy and the Open Economy

D. Sykes Wilford

The Praeger Special Studies program, through a selective worldwide distribution network, makes available to the academic, government, and business communities significant and timely research in U.S. and international economic, social, and political issues.

Monetary Policy and the Open Economy

Mexico's Experience

Praeger Publishers New York London

PRAEGER SPECIAL STUDIES IN INTERNATIONAL ECONOMICS AND DEVELOPMENT

Library of Congress Cataloging in Publication Data

Wilford, D   Sykes.
    Monetary policy and the open economy.

    (Praeger special studies in international economics
and development)
    Bibliography: p.
    Includes index.
    1. Monetary policy—Mexico.   2. Balance of
payments—Mexico.   3. Money supply—Mexico.
4. Fiscal policy—Mexico.   I. Title.
HG665.W54   1977   332.4'972   77-14386
ISBN 0-03-028156-3

PRAEGER SPECIAL STUDIES
200 Park Avenue, New York, N.Y., 10017, U.S.A.

Published in the United States of America in 1977
by Praeger Publishers,
A Division of Holt, Rinehart and Winston, CBS, Inc.

789   038   987654321

Printed in the United States of America

This book is dedicated to my wife, Jane Marie Micholet Wilford. Without her guidance and understanding, I would not have been able to pursue this goal to its conclusion.

In this book the author analyzes the remarkable successes of the Mexican economy in the post-World War II period in adapting to and participating in a generally stable international economic and financial community. While other countries in similar circumstances experienced periodic and traumatic readjustments to the international economy, Mexico maintained both a stable exchange rate with the U.S. dollar, a rate of inflation that mirrored that of the United States, and a very high rate of economic growth over the period of 1955-75. The major thrust of the book is to analyze the role that macroeconomic policies played in this success story and its unhappy ending in the mid-1970s.

The author develops an analytical framework that is based on the original works of Robert Mundell and of the late Harry G. Johnson, whose tragic and premature death occurred earlier this year. The influence of Johnson's works are particularly strong in this book. His emphasis on general equilibrium theory, his successful efforts to theoretically integrate the real and financial sectors in open economies, his great instinct for identifying the important elements of an issue, and his overriding concern for the developing nations are all prominent factors in this study of Mexican development.

Adapting the general theoretical constructs of Harry Johnson and Robert Mundell to the unique policy and institutional experience of Mexico is the author's challenge, and he meets it admirably. He very successfully integrates his detailed analyses of the Mexican fiscal and monetary policy mechanisms and of the Mexican financial system generally, all of which differ importantly in some respects from our own, with the general theoretical concepts of internal and external equilibrium in an open economy on fixed exchange rates. The result on the one hand is a new test of the monetary approach to the balance of payments theory, and on the other a fresh and innovative reexamination of the successes and failures of the Mexican policymakers in the post-World War II period.

Practitioners of the dismal science, to whom all things are not possible, will appreciate the general guidelines that dictated fiscal and monetary policies in Mexico in the postwar period, although some, I believe, will wrongly argue that these policies were aimed too low. As the author interprets these guidelines, fiscal and monetary variables were to be expanded only in proportion to the realized rate of real economic expansion; thus macropolicy largely adapted itself to economic growth rather than the reverse. As the author also shows, these policies worked admirably so long as inflation was low, so that real and nominal growth rates were similar. The author argues convincingly that, in the early 1970s, the same policy guidelines led to serious problems in both government spending and revenue plans, and to the control of domestic money expansion. One result was large savings in the international accounts as both internal and external disequilibria worked themselves out.

Richard Zecher

The nature of monetary policy, its usefulness, and its effects upon certain targets (the money stock, the interest rate, the price level, the balance of payments, the money multiplier, and other domestic variables) depend upon the precise nature of the money supply mechanism. This book addresses itself primarily to answering two questions: To what extent can the domestic monetary authorities in a small, developing, open economy control the money supply? Does the monetary approach to the balance-of-payments hypothesis explain the effects of monetary policy for a small, developing, open economy?

Analysis of the actual course of a particular country's policy is a very useful path to follow when examining any particular theory. At the same time, the importance of a theory's applicability to a particular set of circumstances, and its usefulness as a tool in analyzing both policies and the institutions within which those policies function, cannot be overstressed. The monetary approach is a convenient vehicle by which one can examine the experience and policies in Mexico since the mid-1950s. Using it also provides the opportunity to test the theory as it applies to a small open economy—Mexico.

Mexico has experienced stability and real growth since the mid-1950s. For most of the period since the 1954 devaluation, the Mexican authorities have been careful to maintain a monetary policy consistent with their development goals. Their concern over the exchange rate, economic development, and fiscal responsibility helped to create an economy that by 1973 ranked thirteenth among Western countries in terms of gross domestic product (GDP). By 1972 Mexico was seventeenth in the world in terms of energy consumption and fifteenth in terms of railroad traffic. There is no doubt that the nation will become even more important in the future.

Whether one considers oneself a monetarist or a structuralist, as those labels apply to development economics, one would have to agree that Mexican economic development has been influenced by the policies of the government—both fiscal and monetary authorities. There can be little doubt that development policy helped to create the financial structure within which monetary policy would work. In Mexico, as in most countries, it is difficult to separate monetary from fiscal policy decisions. The interest of this study lies mainly on the monetary side of that nation's theory and institutions; however, for a proper analysis of the monetary process in Mexico we examine, both theoretically and empirically, the fiscal revenue structure and attempt to understand how it influenced monetary policies and institutions.

This book reports the Mexican monetary experience since 1954, utilizing the monetary approach to the balance-of-payments hypothesis as an analytical tool. In the process of the research we explore issues relating to the nature of

Central Bank control over the money supply in Mexico and other institutional questions within which the monetary approach hypothesis may be utilized. Among the specific results of the analysis are that, under a fixed exchange rate, the Central Bank cannot independently set interest rate differentials vis-a-vis world rates at a level sufficiently high to insure foreign reserve inflows; that until recently the Central Bank encouraged a climate such that Mexican risk premiums on debt instruments were lessened; that the Central Bank cannot indefinitely influence the domestic rate of inflation while maintaining a fixed exchange rate; that the Central Bank can control domestically created money; that the Central Bank cannot control, but can influence, foreign reserve positions, and therefore the money supply; and that the Central Bank can control the channels of domestically created money. We further conclude to what extent monetary policy affected the Mexican economic experience with respect to prices, interest rates, the money stock, domestic credit, and foreign reserves for the period 1954–76. Finally, we conclude that various fiscal and monetary policies culminated in a situation that necessitated Central Bank creation of domestic money, with resultant losses of foreign reserves. We argue that pressures on reserves to leave Mexico during 1975 and 1976 were the primary factors leading to the de facto devaluation of the peso.

ACKNOWLEDGMENTS

This study has benefited from many comments by friends and colleagues. Particular thanks must be given to Professor Richard Zecher, who first kindled my interest in this subject and continued to make useful comments at every stage of the work. Gratitude is also extended to Professors J. E. Tanner, Frank Keller, and John Rutledge for comments on the research at various stages. The book has certainly benefited from criticism by various members of the 1975/76 Tulane Workshop; in particular, Professors W. Michael Cox and Bluford H. Putnam provided useful comments on chapters 2, 3, and 4, while discussion on statistical procedures with Professor Charles Smithson were invaluable. Professors Alden Toevs, Jules Lebon, and David T. King provided encouragement and discussion from which the analysis benefited.

I must acknowledge the patient and diligent efforts of my brother, Professor Walton T. Wilford, for his criticism and suggestions throughout the work. Further, I thank the other members of my family, the late Reverend J. D. Wilford, Rebecca Sykes Wilford, Jasper D. Wilford, Jr., and its newest member Jane M. Wilford, for their encouragement and moral support.

Finally, I would like to acknowledge my debt to the individuals mentioned above who are responsible for suggestions that improved the analysis and made this work more complete. However, I did not always follow their advice; therefore, remaining errors and omissions are the responsibility of the author.

CONTENTS

LIST OF TABLES AND FIGURES

Monetary Policy and the Open Economy

1

INTRODUCTION

> I shall therefore venture to acknowledge that not only as a man but as a British subject, I pray for flourishing commerce of Germany, Spain, Italy, and even France itself. I am at least certain that Great Britain, and all of those nations, would flourish more, did their sovereigns and ministers adopt such enlarged and benevolent sentiments towards each other.
>
> David Hume
> "Of the Jealousy of Trade"

Controversy on the effects of monetary policy in a small, developing economy exists in the literature. The nature of monetary policy, its usefulness, and its effects upon certain targets—the money stock, the interest rate, the price level, the balance of payments, the money multiplier, and the other domestic variables—depend upon the precise nature of the money supply mechanism. This study addresses itself to these issues. Knowledge of the control that the authorities may have over domestic variables is a necessary condition for developing appropriate policy. In an economy that is continually advancing in its state of development this information is doubly important. Therefore, whether one is a monetarist or a structuralist is not important in addressing these issues; rather, one need only be concerned with what is an appropriate policy in light of the degree of control one has over particular economic variables.

Since the balance of payments is a very important issue to the policy maker in a developing economy, it is the focal point of this analysis—necessarily the issue is broad enough to include other variables in the discussion. Certainly fiscal policy affects the balance of payments; development policies in many ways determine how fiscal policy is initiated and implemented, thereby affecting the balance of payments. However, we feel that the balance of payments can be directly determined by the incipient state of excess demand for money—a hypothesis derived from the monetary approach to the balance of payments. This does not say that fiscal policy has little or no effect on components of the balance of payments; what this approach provides is a theoretical framework within which we can analyze the balance of payments. In the course of the analysis, a thorough examination of fiscal and development policies is necessary in order to understand how and why the incipient state of excess demand for money explains reserve flows.

In a small, open economy on a fixed exchange rate, the balance of payments, through its contributions to the monetary base, is a key mechanism for achieving monetary equilibrium. For instance, suppose the supply of domestically created money exceeds demand. The excess supply of money leads people to readjust their portfolios by purchasing goods and services or bonds, in order to return to equilibrium. Within a system of fixed exchange rates, domestic demanders can purchase foreign currencies from the Central Bank in order to obtain goods and services or bonds from abroad so as to attain portfolio equilibrium. Reserves leave the country, thereby lowering the money stock until monetary equilibrium is reestablished. In this sense, one may conclude that the balance of payments is a monetary phenomenon. Of course, there remains room within the theory to examine how all of the pertinent monetary variables are determined. Some of the policy factors that affect the monetary variables directly addressed in the analysis are fiscal in nature. Thus, the monetary approach to the balance of payments provides a convenient theoretical and empirical framework within which the economist can analyze fiscal as well as monetary developments in a small, open economy—specifically, Mexico.

There are four major reasons for the choice of Mexico. First, it is a small country and maintained until the fall of 1976 a fixed exchange rate with the United States since the 1954 peso devaluation. Second, though considered an underdeveloped country by many economists, Mexico has a well-developed financial structure with a Central Bank interested in maintaining a satisfactory balance of payments and in promoting development. Third, the policies of the last seven years which led to the devaluation of the Mexican peso offer fertile ground for application of the monetary approach framework. Fourth, Mexico is in close geographic proximity to the United States. Notable for our purpose is the fact that a majority of Mexico's foreign investors are American, and much of its trade is with the United States. Such a relationship is especially useful, since the United States may serve as a proxy for the rest of the world in the empirical comparisons.

The two general issues relating to the exogenous or endogenous nature of the money stock of the Mexican economy may be addressed by evaluating its empirical experience since 1954. On the one hand, if the money stock for Mexico is determined exogenously, a specific set of monetary policies is implied— for example, the "monetarist" stance with respect to monetary policy. On the other hand, if money stock is endogenously determined, policy implications are quite different. Thus, a central issue that requires resolution by Mexican policy makers is whether the variables that affect the money stock are endogenously or exogenously determined. The techniques utilized for empirical investigation of the control maintained by policy makers over the stock are derived from the general hypothesis of the monetary approach to the balance of payments. This approach will not assume, a priori, that money is endogenously or exogenously determined, but will incorporate specified money demand and supply equations to test the relationship between foreign reserve flows and changes in both money demand and variables determining money supply. The analysis occurs under conditions of long-run equilibrium in money supply and money demand. The relation of these money demand and money supply variables to foreign reserve positions will permit inference vis-a-vis the exogenous or endogenous nature of the stock of money. This follows from the fact that the stock of high-powered money in Mexico has been historically determined largely by foreign reserves.

This book includes seven chapters. Chapter 1 is the introduction. Chapter 2 contains a historical perspective of Mexico, a review of the literature, money demand and money supply equations, and alternative specifications of the reserve flow model of the monetary approach to the balance of payments. Chapter 3 presents empirical results for tests of price and interest rate assumptions of the monetary model, as well as tests of different model specifications. In Chapter 4 we empirically examine the fiscal revenue structure of Mexico in order to provide a basis for the framework within which monetary policy is implemented. Chapter 5 develops the institutional framework for examining prices, interest rates, foreign reserves, domestic credit, and the money multiplier. We analyze those variables by drawing upon the empirical results of Chapter 2 and the policy actions of the Mexican monetary policy makers since the 1954 devaluation. Chapter 6 describes in detail, by period, the actions of the Mexican monetary policy makers since 1954, including the policy relevant to the 1976 devaluation. Chapter 7 summarizes some of the conclusions of the study.

CHAPTER
2

BALANCE OF PAYMENTS IN MEXICO: INSTITUTIONS, LITERATURE REVIEW, AND THE MONETARY MODEL

The analysis of this chapter can trace its roots across time to some of the earliest writings on economic matters. The balance of payments, prices, and money have been a part of man's thinking since the Middle Ages. In his *Résponse et paradoxes de malistroit*, printed in 1569, Jean Boudin discusses the evolution of prices in the sixteenth century. Of note, he talks about the supply of money and the effects of exports on prices. During the late Middle Ages the "bullionists" were eager to maintain a nation's wealth through preserving treasure—gold (money). Gerald Malyner, one of the most important members of this school, was concerned with the true parity of foreign exchanges and discussed the determination of the parity of exchange as it related to bullion (international reserves) flows. Thomas Mann later developed a theory of trade, reserves, and money. The mercantilists centered their economic thinking on maintaining a positive balance of payments so as to build wealth.

These intellectuals broke the ground for economists who are today concerned with money and the balance of payments. It was the Scottish philosopher David Hume in the mid-eighteenth century, however, who formulated a theory of the balance of payments that is the basis of the contemporary theory. It was based upon a relationship of prices, money stocks, international reserve flows, and automatic adjustment. Although different in certain aspects, Hume's key idea of the balance of payments as a part of an automatically adjusting industrial economic system is at the core of the monetary approach to the balance of payments.

This chapter reviews a monetary approach to the balance-of-payments theory based on work by Robert Mundell, Harry Johnson, and Richard Zecher. The theory is advanced as it specifically relates to Mexico, and therefore a summary of relevant facts about recent Mexican economic history is presented.

After this short aside, the development of the theory of the monetary approach to the balance of payments is presented.

MEXICO'S MACROECONOMIC GROWTH TRENDS

Mexico's economic development since 1954 is a story of success. Seen by many as the Japan of Latin America, Mexico's real gross national product (GNP) has increased at an annual rate of 6 percent since 1940, and per capita GNP growth has averaged 2.5 percent.[1] Per capita income reached approximately $700 in 1970. No other Latin American country has rivaled Mexico's growth rate since 1954, although Brazil has recently made considerable strides.

Further, investigation of cost-of-living indexes since 1954 shows that Mexico has among the lowest rates of inflation in the subhemisphere. Indeed, until recently Mexico's inflation rate has been comparable with that of the United States and Western Europe while other Latin American nations, notably Argentina, Brazil, and Chile, experienced hyperinflation. The Mexican peso was devalued on Easter weekend in 1954 and remained pegged at 12.49 pesos per United States dollar until September 1, 1976.

The Mexican economy, like those of most Latin American countries, has been traditionally tied to the foreign sector. Along with other major Latin nations, Mexico accepted Raul Prebisch's thesis that the terms of trade for developing nations decline over time with respect to the developed nations.[2] Along with the distortions in trade created by World War II, Mexico's adherence to the Prebisch thesis induced it to accept import substitution as a development policy. Though the share of commodity imports has not diminished appreciably since 1940, its composition has changed. With the application of selective tariff controls, capital imports have increased at the expense of consumer goods. The export sector shows the effect of import-substitution policies, with manufactured goods claiming an increased absolute and relative share. At the same time agricultural exports increased dramatically in the 1950s with the introduction of more advanced production methods, although neglect of the agricultural sector during the late 1960s reversed this trend. Tourism and U.S. border transactions also have risen as a percentage of exports. The growth of these commodities and services as a share of exports appears to have been at the expense of a declining silver and gold industry. Though manufacturing and agriculture increased as a proportion of exports, total commodity exports declined in the 1950s with the shift to protectionism implied by a policy of import substitution. Accompanying this policy were balance-of-trade deficits that were financed through tourism and foreign borrowing.

The "Mexican Miracle" has not been without problems. The protectionism introduced in the 1950s has reduced dependence upon imported consumer goods, but replaced it with dependence upon capital imports. The industrial state imposes new problems, such as urbanization and the auxiliary economic resources required to service such a society. As with most of the Western world, the 1970s have produced greater inflation and economic instability in Mexico. In 1971 the growth rate of real income fell to less than 4 percent, the lowest since 1954, while prices rose at an annual rate of 5 percent. Finally, in 1976 Mexico experienced depreciation of its national currency, inflation, and weakened real growth.

MEXICO'S RELEVANT MONETARY HISTORY

Mexico's economic growth "miracle" occurred, for most of the period, in a climate of financial stability. GNP has by and large increased steadily, with minor fluctuations in phase with those of the United States—per capita income increased from U.S.$150 in 1953 to approximately U.S.$700 in 1970. The ensuing examination of the monetary variable aggregates reflects this stability.

Prices

Until recently, prices were relatively stable, increasing at an annual rate of 3 percent for the period 1956-70, compared with a 7 percent annual rate for the 15-year period prior to 1955. Most Mexican economists attribute the low inflation rate to decreased public expenditure as a percentage of national output. Since much of the public expenditure deficits were financed by money creation, the rate of money creation required for such financing declined as a percentage of national output over most of the period. Further, alternative financing has been utilized through the regional development of a financial system that systematically moves private savings to the public sector. Gilberto Escobedo states: "Monetary authorities have found new means to finance government expenditures so as to neutralize overexpansionary action derived from this expenditure or from foreign sources."[3]

Real Investment

Real investment, both public and private, rose at approximately 17 percent per annum between 1954 and 1974. Public investment was directed primarily to heavy capital formation, which accounts for approximately 45 percent of total Mexican investment. Public investment was financed through various techniques, including taxation, domestic borrowing through financial intermediaries, direct domestic bond issuance, foreign bond issuance, direct foreign borrowing, and money creation. The tax system was designed to promote private investment through fiscal incentives, thereby reducing the potential amounts from fiscal sources that might be directed to financing public investment (see Chapter 5).

Through increased savings in the private sector and a system of fractional reserves, Mexican monetary authorities have been able to borrow private savings for government investment by utilizing required reserves on deposits in financial institutions. Monetary authorities have been asked, consequently, to finance expenditures through the private (as well as public) banking system rather than rely solely upon creation of new money. Economists have suggested that the policy makes the government dependent upon the private and public financial institutions for its deficit financing, although money supply growth was indeed limited to a rate comparable with the rate of growth of nominal GNP through the 1950s and 1960s.[4] More recently these traditional sources of funds have not been able to finance an increasing deficit, so money creation has become a principal source of funds.

Velocity

The velocity of circulation* has exhibited little annual variability since 1960, although it has declined from about 14 in 1962 to 8.1 in 1975. Thus, since velocity declined slowly, increasing the money supply at a rate comparable with or slightly greater than growth in real output would have been consistent with a noninflationary monetary policy.

Multiplier

The money multiplier[†] for M_1 was also stable over the period 1954-70. During the 1970s it became less stable, falling dramatically in 1972 and 1973. Though the narrow definition of money (M_1) is employed, thus placing emphasis on money as a medium of exchange, a broader definition that includes interest-paying deposits (M_2) suggests less stability for both the velocity and the multiplier during this period.[5]

---

*Velocity (V) is defined as $V = Y/M_1$ where M_1 = currency and coins in circulation + demand deposits and Y = gross domestic product. For an analysis of velocity movements in Mexico, see D. Sykes Wilford, "The Velocity of Money and Financial Development in Mexico," working paper, Federal Reserve Bank of New York, 1977.

†The money multiplier (a) = M_1/H where H = high-powered money.

External Sector

Mexico's external sector has changed in structure since the mid-1950s, with import-substitution policies altering the composition in favor of capital, as opposed to consumer, imports. Capital imports have averaged an annual growth rate of 18 percent, much above the rate of growth in GNP. Furthermore, their rate of increase has been far above the annual rate of growth of exports. The resulting current-account deficit has been met through foreign financing, direct investment, and credits. The inflow of foreign funds has allowed overall reserves to increase even with a declining balance of trade.

Gilberto Escobedo notes:

> ... external funds take the form of either loans or direct foreign investments. The latter one, not available for government's deficit financing, has been following a steadily growing trend in the last fifty years.
>
> This source of funds [foreign loans], besides helping to finance the current account deficit of the balance of payments, can be used to finance government deficit. The expedient used is the legal reserve requirements which are imposed on commercial as well as investment banks.

Furthermore, Escobedo writes:

> If the amount of the foreign funds available were enough to finance the current account deficit of the balance of payments, the central bank would be in a neutral position; that is, neither expanding or reducing international reserves.
>
> If, however, the net domestic credit of the Banco de Mexico had to be expanded over its neutral level to finance a government deficit, compensatory action would have to be taken reducing credit to banks, so that the position of international reserves would remain unchanged. Otherwise, this expansion would lead to a reduction of international reserves in order to balance the deficit in current account, endangering the goals of stable rates and free convertibility.[6]

These statements by Escobedo suggest that the goal of monetary authorities is to maintain real income growth with stable exchange rates. The techniques employed were, for much of the period, consistent with the monetary approach to the balance-of-payments theory.

REVIEW OF THEORETICAL LITERATURE
ON MONETARY BALANCE OF PAYMENTS

Although the view that the balance of payments is essentially a monetary phenomenon is relatively new, its rationale can be traced to David Hume's discussion of the price specie-flow mechanism. Hume argued that a country's stock of money could be adjusted exactly to the demand for money in that country through surpluses or deficits in the balance of payments.

Though Hume's work is basically the forerunner of the modern monetary approach, it differs in a number of respects. Major theoretical works on the balance of payments were essentially elaborations of Hume's analysis until the 1930s. While Hume's theory rested on automatic adjustment, the Keynesian revolution of the 1930s postulated a theoretical framework that challenged the assumptions of automatic adjustment and replaced it with the view that the balance of payments was a policy problem of the government. Harry Johnson notes:

> On the Keynesian assumptions of wage rigidity, a devaluation would change the real prices of domestic goods relative to foreign goods in the foreign and domestic markets, thereby promoting substitutions in production and consumption. On Keynesian assumptions of mass unemployment, any repercussions of these substitutions on the demand for domestic output would be assumed to be met by variations in output and employment and repercussions of such variations onto the balance of payments regarded as secondary. Finally, on the same assumption together with the general Keynesian denigration of the influence of money on the economy and concentration on the short-run, the connections between the balance of payments and the money supply and aggregate demand could be disregarded.[7]

Other economists in the Keynesian and post-Keynesian periods have discussed balance of payments primarily in light of trade theory while relegating the monetary sector to a secondary role.[8]

Although there has been relatively little theoretical and empirical work on the role of money in international trade, J. E. Meade in the early 1950s, J. J. Polak in 1957, and Robert Mundell in the 1960s began stressing its influence on managing the balance of payments.[9] Mundell has stressed the proper mix of monetary and fiscal policy in simultaneously achieving balance of payments and full employment. According to him, one may use these two policy instruments for different objectives, with monetary policy having a more significant effect than fiscal policy on the external sector.

Following Mundell's seminal 1968 work, several economists have contributed to the literature on monetary approach to the balance of payments, including Harry Johnson, Richard Zecher, Bijan Aghevli, M. G. Porter, John Rutledge, M. S. Khan, A. K. Swoboda, and Hans Genberg.[10]

While the monetary approach is gaining theoretical support in the literature, empirical work has just begun. Indeed, there have been few applications of the model to an emerging country. Mundell, Johnson, and Jacob Frenkel and Carlos Rodríguez have dealt mainly with the theoretical implications of the model. Johnson notes that monetary models of the balance of payments are basically simple because they concentrate on the overall balance of payments while ignoring individual accounts and possible changes in the structure of payments over time.[11] Though simple, the basic monetary models are logically derived, given the view that the balance of payments is essentially a monetary phenomenon. Aghevli and Khan state:

> In the framework of the monetary approach, the balance of payments position of a country is considered a reflection of decisions on the part of its residents to accumulate or run down their stock of money balances. It is this process of adjustment to the desired stock of money balances that results in balances of payments deficits and surpluses.[12]

In this framework Aghevli and Khan are speaking of a balance of payments that is best defined (under a fixed-exchange-rate regime or, more loosely, under a "dirty-floating" system) as the rate of change in international reserves held by a country or, more specifically, held by its monetary authorities in order to provide or absorb foreign exchange in the event of an ex ante excess demand or supply. Thus, the monetary approach says that the balance of payments must be related through an identity relationship to monetary factors that are expressed in the supply of and demand for money.

Given world mobility of capital and goods, combined with the assumptions of a fixed exchange rate, the importation and exportation of capital from a small country will not affect prices. Prices are determined exogenously by world prices. The nominal interest rate is also fixed exogenously by the world rate. Therefore, any excess demand for money in the internal sector must be met by an increase in the domestic money stock through domestic credit augmented by inflows of foreign reserves. If one assumes that the domestic money supply is not increased to meet the new demand for funds, there will automatically be an increase in international reserves or a balance-of-payments surplus. The channel by which the excess funds arrive is of no importance here, since the issue is the final balance-of-payments position and not the means by which the surplus is generated—that is, the current or capital account.

In short, the model assumes that prices are determined exogenously, that the domestic interest rate is equal to the world rate, and that the country is at general-equilibrium full employment.* The first two premises follow from the assumptions of mobility of goods and services between countries in the goods market and freely flowing funds in the capital market. Johnson notes that this model does not suggest the money illusion that some of the more standard models require for adjustment.[13] Clearly, given a fixed exchange rate, the assumption of world price arbitrage denies the necessity of money illusion for adjustment. Further, the assumption of full employment is defensible on the ground that the monetary approach deals essentially with the long run. The relationship between excess demand for money balances and the balance of payments implies that an increase in real income leads to increased demand for real cash balances, thus generating an inflow of foreign reserves. Therefore, contrary to both the standard Keynesian models and the Hume specie-flow mechanism, economic growth will generate an inflow of foreign reserves. The growth leads to increased money demand by raising real income, ceteris paribus, and will be positively related to reserve movements.†

The Hume specie-flow mechanism, on the other hand, implies that growth in real income will generate increased demand, causing a rise in prices of domestically produced goods in the home country. This generates an eventual reserve outflow as domestic demand for imports increases. The reduced money stock associated with the reserve outflow will then lower income and prices to equilibrium. This argument does suggest adjustments of reserves to excess demand or supply of money, but adjustment through the goods market without consideration of the capital account. Furthermore, all money is considered to be outside money, on the assumption that there is no Central Bank capable of creating moneys that are not backed by international reserves. Hume also appeals to relative price changes as his mechanism for adjustment where the monetary model allows prices to be determined exogenously.

The monetary model is therefore similar to the Hume model in that they both have automatic adjustment mechanisms. However, they differ in that the monetary approach permits reserve balances to adjust directly to excess demand and supply of money instead of to the relative price movements postulated by

---

*A less rigid assumption, sufficient for our analysis, is that the balance of payments does not affect real output.

†Richard Zecher comments: "This result may appear to be at variance with the absorption theory in which rising income increases imports and generates reserve outflows. However, the absorption theory is concerned with the balance of trade rather than the balance of payments. Whatever the effects on the balance of trade, rapid growth does appear on a casual basis to be associated with reserve inflows (Japan, Germany), and slow growth with reserve outflows (U.S.A., U.K.)." See his "Monetary Equilibrium and International Reserve Flows in Australia," *Journal of Finance* 29 (December 1974): 1325.

classical theory. The monetary approach is thus a theory meaning, in stationary equilibrium, that money supply is equal to money demand, the balance of payments is zero, and domestic credit cannot be changing. However, in a dynamic economy with a changing money demand (possibly due to real growth in output) the static relationship allows one to observe the change in reserves, as a result of exogenous influences in the movement from one equilibrium point to another. The automatic nature of the adjustment mechanism allows one to concentrate on the causes of reserve flows by examining monetary factors, since, as A. K. Swoboda points out, "balance of payments disequilibrium must, of necessity, be transitory in nature" unless continuously caused by exogenous shocks (such as continuous changes in domestically created money in a stationary economy or by growth in a nonstationary economy).[14] Finally, it should be noted that the monetary approach is a theory based on the long run. It only tells us what the effect of a shock on stability will be after adjustment has taken place, but does not concentrate on how that adjustment occurs. Thus, one is provided with a method of analyzing the balance of payments by concentrating on the money market.

THE MONETARY MODEL

The monetary model as formulated by Johnson and Zecher may be defined in eight basic equations. The stock of high-powered money is related to the money supply in the identity statement

$$M = a \cdot H \tag{1}$$

where M = money supply, a = money multiplier, and H = stock of high-powered money (coins and currency in circulation plus bank deposits at the Central Bank).

The monetary authority's balance sheet appears as follows:

Assets	Liabilities
R	H
OA	OL

where R = international reserves, OA = assets of monetary authority other than R, and OL = liabilities other than high-powered money. For example, R is made up of gold, foreign currencies, and Special Drawing Rights (SDRs), while OA is composed of bonds from the private and public sectors, loans, and other items, and OL is made up of Treasury and public deposits at the Central Bank, and other liabilities.

Therefore,

$$H = R + (OA - OL) = R + D \tag{2}$$

where

$$D = OA - OL = \text{domestic credit}$$

Substituting (2) into (1), we derive a new money supply function:

$$M = a \cdot (R + D) \tag{3}$$

Zecher postulates a money demand equation in the form

$$(M/P) = \frac{y^{a_1} e}{i^{a_2}} \tag{4}$$

where

P = the price index
y = real income
i = the rate of interest
e = a log normally distributed stochastic disturbance term.

Assuming that money demand is homogeneous of degree 1 in prices, (4) is rewritten as

$$M = \frac{P y^{a_1} e}{i^{a_2}} \tag{5}$$

Since $M = a \cdot (R + D)$, then

$$a \cdot (R + D) = \frac{P y^{a_1} e}{i^{a_2}} \tag{6}$$

We are interested in percentage changes in the variables, so a transformation is necessary. That is,

$$\ln a + \ln (R + D) = \ln P + a_1 \ln y - a_2 \ln i + \ln e \tag{7}$$

Differentiating (7) with respect to time,

$$\frac{1}{a}\frac{da}{dt} + \frac{1}{R+D}\frac{d(R+D)}{dt} = \frac{1}{P}\frac{dP}{dt} + \frac{a_1}{y}\frac{dy}{dt} - \frac{a_2}{i}\frac{di}{dt} + \frac{1}{e}\frac{de}{dt}$$

and defining $gx = \frac{1}{x}\frac{dx}{dt}$ where x = a, R, D, y, P, and i yields

$$ga + \frac{R}{R+D} gR + \frac{D}{R+D} gD = gP + a_1 gy - a_2 gi + e'$$

where $e' = \frac{1}{e} \frac{de}{dt}$.

From (2)

$$ga + (R/H)gR + (D/H) gD = gP + a_1 gy - a_2 gi + e'$$

Defining $(R/H)gR$ as the dependent variable, then

$$(R/H)gR = a_1 gy - a_2 gi + gP - ga - (D/H) gD + e' \tag{8}$$

As is evident in equation (8), the variation in the foreign reserves held depends upon the percentage change in income (gy), the percentage change in the interest rate (gi), the percentage change in the price level (gP), the percentage change in the money multiplier (ga), and the percentage change in domestic credit (gD) multiplied by D/H. This follows from equation (3), which shows that a change in the money stock can come through a change in a, H, or R.

As noted earlier, a positive a_1 is anticipated because income is positively related to reserve flow via the money demand equation. Further, domestic credit is negatively related to reserve flows. Both of these conclusions are in disagreement with one or more Keynesian theories of the balance of payments.*

The relationship of domestic credit to international reserves in the monetary model offers a policy outline that is quite straightforward for increasing foreign reserves. A contraction in the domestic money supply will necessarily cause reserve inflow (assuming other variables to be constant). Therefore, to correct a negative balance of payments, the policy strategist should be concerned with keeping domestic credit, ceteris paribus, expanding at a slower rate than that of money demand. The nature of the model is, as Johnson remarked, simple. The fact that it ignores some of the channels of reserve creation does not distract from its theoretical and empirical usefulness.

---

*Harry Johnson points out that the monetary model may be contrasted with various Keynesian theories on growth and the balance of payments. He notes that one theory suggests that growth usually leads to reserve outflows (completely ignoring the effects of demand for money) while the other suggests "domestic credit expansion will improve the balance of payments by stimulating investment and productivity increases and thereby lowering domestic prices in relation to foreign prices and improving the current account through the resulting substitutions of domestic for foreign goods in the foreign and domestic markets." Harry Johnson, *Further Essays in Monetary Economics* (Cambridge, Mass.: Harvard University Press, 1973), p. 240.

THEORETICAL SPECIFICATIONS

This section analyzes three principal theoretical concepts for Mexico with relation to the monetary approach to the balance of payments: the demand for money, the supply of money, and the demand for foreign reserves. A series of models is presented, using as a point of departure the literature of Johnson, Zecher, Aghevli, Khan, Milton Friedman, John Deavers, Philip Cagan, Karl Brunner, and Allan Meltzer.[15]

The Demand for Money

The purpose of this section is to determine the theoretical specifications of the demand for real and nominal money in Mexico. While money demand analysis has been undertaken by several economists, one of the more successful studies was by Philip Cagan in 1956.[16] Though primarily interested in hyperinflation, Cagan offers insights into why individuals hold money. In addition, Friedman's analysis on money demand is helpful in specifying the appropriate money demand variables.[17] By utilizing their work along with that of others, the proper specification of money demand in Mexico is derived.

The fact that the demand for money is an integral part of the monetary approach to the balance of payments may be illustrated by reference to equation (4), a real-money demand equation that takes the form

$$(M/P) = y^{a_1} e / i^{a_2} \qquad\qquad (9)$$

where

P = the price index
y = real permanent income
i = the rate of interest
e = a log normally distributed stochastic disturbance term.

The resulting theoretical equation for reserve flows derived from (9) is given by

$$(R/H)gR = a_1 gy - a_2 gi + gP - ga - (D/H)gD + e$$

Thus, final specification of the reserve flow equation depends upon the definition of money demand. It is therefore necessary to develop further the Mexican money demand relationship prior to specifying the appropriate reserve flow equation for the nation.

There are a number of models in money demand theory that may be utilized to postulate a money demand equation. The real demand for money (M^d/P) is a function of several key variables. The Cambridge equation shows that (money/prices) = (ky/prices) where k = 1/V and V is velocity. As a result (M^d/P) = f(y, V); that is, real money balance is positively related to real income (y) and to the inverse of velocity. What are the factors determining V, and what, therefore, will stimulate changes in k? It is this change in k that is critical to money demand analysis and, as Deavers notes, is typical of the "simple way that characterizes modern quantity theory approach."[18]

Several variables affect k. In analyzing money demand under conditions of rapid inflation, Deavers and Cagan show that the cost of holding money motivated individuals to alter their real money balances. If the rate of inflation rises, one expects individuals, according to Deavers and Cagan, to economize on real money balances as the cost of holding these balances increases. Since those holding monetary balances adjust them to the anticipated costs of holding money, the appropriate cost variable determining the amount of money demanded is the expected cost of holding an asset. In the case of money, the expected cost is the anticipated rate of inflation. Other variables that would fully specify a money demand equation, according to Friedman, would encompass the nominal return on bonds and equities, the ratio of human to nonhuman wealth, and individual tastes and preferences.[19]

A fully specified money demand equation is, therefore,

$$\frac{M^d}{P} = f\left(y, \pi^*, i_B, i_E, \frac{W_N}{W_h}, t\right) \tag{10}$$

where

i_B = rate of return on bonds
i_E = rate of return on equities
W_N/W_h = ratio of nonhuman to human wealth
t = tastes and preferences
π^* = anticipated rate of inflation.

This enumeration of independent variables may be utilized to specify the appropriate money demand equation for Mexico. Lack of data on the ratio of nonhuman to human wealth, and on tastes and preferences, requires that these be eliminated from the money demand equation. Because of questionable reliability of meaningful interest rate data in most underdeveloped countries, the relatively primitive state of financial market structures, and government intervention in the money market through mandatory subsidized credit quotas, it is difficult to construct a reliable estimator of nominal interest rates over time.

The assumption of the model, however, implies that the rate of interest in Mexico actually reflects the world rate of interest. Under this assumption, the rate of return on Mexican bonds is included in the money demand equation.

The empirical validity of the above theoretical specifications depends largely upon the availability of reliable data. The reported rates of return on bonds in Mexico are not viewed by this researcher as representative. Further, there is no reported series on the rate of return of equities. A proxy series, the index of industrial share prices, could possibly be utilized in the empirical investigation. The adequacy of both the rate of return data on bonds and the industrial share price index data are subject to some criticism. However, the issue is largely an empirical question of the reliability of reported data. Earlier studies on money demand in emerging nations have usually found the reported rate of interest on securities to be statistically insignificant. These results leave inconclusive the influence of interest rates on money demand, and are attributed more to insufficiency of adequate data than to theoretical misspecification.[20]

The utilization of the industrial share price index as a proxy for the rate of return on capital is even more suspect. Though the data from this index are good, the number of shares traded on the Mexican exchange for the period of study is small if compared with total transactions of the exchange. Indeed, the main function of the exchange is to clear bond transactions rather than to deal with equity issues.

The empirical work of this research is addressed to, among other issues, the rate of return dilemma for Mexico as it relates to demand for money.

The variable selected to measure the expected costs of holding money is π, the expected rate of inflation. There are several possible methodological procedures to calculate this variable. While Aghveli and Khan implicitly assume that individuals will make decisions about the costs of holding money that are based on the present rate of inflation,* the method is theoretically deficient for time-series analysis. Deavers suggests that the cost of holding money may be calculated by taking a weighted average (geometrically declining lag structure) of past inflation as an approximation of anticipated inflation.† Cagan builds a series on expected cost from a model by assuming that individuals alter their expectations of future inflation on the basis of mistakes that they have made in the past. While this method is mathematically more appealing than Deavers's, it is, at the same time, more restrictive, in that the function relating weights of the various periods is predetermined by the approach itself.

Alternatively, one may calculate the expected rate of inflation by assuming optimal use of available information to the individual. John Rutledge, in *A*

---

*It is only fair to note that this study employed cross-sectional data. B. J. Aghevli and M. S. Khan, "The Monetary Approach to the Balance of Payments Determination," paper presented at American Economic Association convention, December 1974, pp. 1–10.

†Deavers states, "Call the expected rate of inflation in period t, C. If P_{t-1} and W_1 are the actual rate and its weight in period $t - 1$, and $W_0\ W_1\ W_2 \cdots W_n$, then we have $C_t = P_{t-1}W_i/W_i$." See John Deavers, "The Chilean Inflation and the Demand for Money," in David M. Meiselman, ed., *Varieties of Monetary Experience* (Chicago: University of Chicago Press, 1970), p. 26.

Monetarist Model of Inflationary Expectations, provides alternative models for calculating the expected rate of inflation.[21] One method proposed by Rutledge to calculate the expected rate of inflation is the rational expectation model. This permits prediction of the rate of inflation by examining past growth in money and prices for a closed economy.

Assume a relationship such that the expected rate of inflation (π^*) is dependent upon both the money supply and past or realized inflation. Further, assume that past rates of inflation, as well as rates of growth, affect the money supply with a distributed lag. Then

$$\pi^* = f((L)M_{t-1}(L)\pi_{t-1}) \tag{11}$$

where M = money, π = past rates of inflation, L is the lag operator, and the tth period is the present period.

The practical calculation of the variable π_t entails defining the mathematical structure of the function and solving for π_t. Let

$$\pi_t^* = \pi_t + \epsilon_t \tag{12}$$

and

$$\pi_{t+1}^* = \beta_0 + \beta_1(L)M_{t-1} + \beta_2(L)\pi_{t-1} \tag{13}$$

Transforming equation (13) yields

$$\pi_{t+1} = \pi_{t+1}^* - \epsilon_{t+1} \tag{14}$$

Substituting (13) into (14), one obtains

$$\pi_{t+1} = \beta_0 + \beta_1(L)M_{t-1} + \beta_2(L')\pi_{t-1} - \epsilon_{t+1} \tag{15}$$

Estimating equation (15) will permit solution for parameters β_0, β_1, and β_2. With these specified, one may calculate π_{t+1}^* by means of equation (13).[22]

Empirically, it is important how individuals will allow expectations of inflation to enter the model. Clearly, for a closed economy in a rapidly inflating economy, π^* is a very important variable for empirically examining the demand for money. However, Mexico is an open economy that experienced only slight inflation in 1959-71. Only in the 1970s, as was the case with the United States, did inflation become above 2-4 percent. Since Mexico is an open economy (with a fixed exchange rate), the anticipated long-run rate of inflation would incorporate world information. Given the fact that world anticipation of inflation is captured in the nominal interest rate, the inclusion of π^* in an empirical investigation is not meaningful (empirical evidence found by the author tends to support the case). Therefore, in this study π^*, as an explicit variable in the money demand function, is not considered.

As a result, the specified real money demand model for Mexico includes measures of real income, the cost of holding money, and the real rate of return on investment through the rate of return on bonds; that is

$$\frac{M^d}{P} = f(y, i_B) \tag{16}$$

Selecting a log-linear form for the real money demand equation, we have

$$\frac{M^d}{P} = \frac{y^{a_1} e}{i_B{}^{a_2}} \tag{17}$$

where e is a log-linearly distributed error term and the a's are the elasticities of their respective variables. Since equation (17) represents real money demand, nominal money demand may be expressed as

$$M^d = \frac{y^{a_1} P^{\beta_1} e}{i_B{}^{a_2}} \tag{18}$$

We assume linear homogeneity of degree 1 in the price level for money demand, so the value of β_1 is anticipated to be +1.

Taking the logarithm of equations (16) and (17), we obtain

$$\ln (M^d/P) = a_1 \ln y - a_2 \ln i_B + e \tag{19}$$

and

$$\ln M^d = a_1 \ln y - a_2 \ln i_B + \beta_1 \ln P + e \tag{20}$$

respectively.

Now differentiating with respect to time, equations (19) and (20) become

$$g(M/P) = a_1 gy - a_2 gi_B + e \tag{21}$$

$$gM = a_1 gy - a_2 gi_B + \beta_1 gP + e \tag{22}$$

where $gx = \dfrac{1}{x}\dfrac{dx}{dt}$; x = y, i, and P.

In equation (22) the anticipated sign of a_1 and β_1 is positive, while the sign of a_2 is expected to be negative. This follows from expectations of individual reaction in distributing wealth portfolios optimally. As the rate of return on bonds and equities increases, individuals rearrange their portfolios. Since money is not the only form of wealth, when wealth portfolios are diversified optimally, a change in one of the rates of return on alternative assets will change money demand.[23] Similarly, an increase in the expected rate of inflation will motivate individuals to decrease their real money balances relative to other assets. An increase in real income will have the opposite effect, since individuals, through their increased real income position, can maintain higher balances of all assets. The nominal demand for money equation will have the same expected signs for its independent variables, with the signs of the coefficient gP being +1. This follows from the assumption of homogeneity of degree 1 in prices for equation (18).

Given the proper theoretical specification of money demand in Mexico, then the money supply equation is required for stating an equilibrium relationship. From the balance sheet of the authorities,

$$M \equiv a \cdot H \qquad \text{where } H \equiv R + D$$

This relationship defines the basic money supply equation of the monetary approach to the balance of payments. To relate money supply to money demand and derive the reserve flow equation, one must first analyze money supply in Mexico.

The Supply of Money

One may postulate, on the basis of a fractional reserve system for commercial banks, the balance sheet relationship[24]

$$D^P = \bar{R} + E$$

where

D^P = demand deposits
$\bar{R}$ = bank reserves
E = earning assets.

Thus $D^P/\bar{R} = 1 + E/\bar{R}$. Let $r = \bar{R}/D^P$ where r = the reserve ratio. Thus, given a fractional reserve system, the banking system may create a money stock equivalent to the amount of reserves times its multiplier, $(1/r)$. Since banks must hold required reserves, by law total reserves may be divided into two parts: required and excess. Let r^d represent the legal reserve ratio, and e the ratio of excess reserves (reserves held above those legally required) to deposits. Therefore

$r = r^d + e$ and $1/r = 1/r^d + e$, where r is the bank reserve ratio. Two determinants of the money multiplier are thus the required reserve ratio established by legislation and the Central Bank, and the portfolio desires of the banking community. The way individuals desire to allocate their holdings of money, either as currency or as demand deposits, is expressed as the currency-deposit ratio, K, where $K = C^P/D^P$. The reserve ratio, as a result, gives an incomplete picture of the multiplier effect of a movement in foreign reserves (or domestic credit) on money creation. Adding K to the equation, the money multiplier (a) is

$$a = \frac{1 + K}{(r^d + e) + K} \tag{23}$$

and

$$\frac{\partial a}{\partial r^d} < 0, \quad \frac{\partial a}{\partial e} < 0, \quad \frac{\partial a}{\partial K} < 0$$

Since $M_1 = a \cdot H$ and $a = \dfrac{1 + K}{(r^d + e) + K}$, then

$$\frac{\partial M_1}{\partial r^d} < 0, \quad \frac{\partial M_1}{\partial e} < 0, \quad \frac{\partial M_1}{\partial K} < 0$$

Then, M_1 * is stated as

$$M_1 = \frac{1 + K}{(r^d + e) + K} \cdot H \tag{24}$$

where high-powered or base money (H) may be defined by looking at its sources. High-powered money is an asset of the financial sector that is supplied by the Central Bank and the government treasury. In Mexico these assets are determined by the balance sheet of the Central Bank. The required reserve, r^d, is a government policy variable. Finally, e is determined by the financial intermediaries and K is a public allocation variable.

An Alternative Approach to D

An alternative definition of domestic credit as analyzed by G. H. Borts and J. A. Hanson is $\Delta D \equiv (Y_g - t - i_b)$, where the sources of government funds, including taxes (t) and government debt (i_b), are subtracted from government

---

*As defined, M_1 includes coin and currency in circulation plus noninterest-bearing deposits. See Figures 3.1 and 3.2 for historical movements in money and its components.

expenditures (Y_g).[25] The remainder (ΔD) must be domestically created credit— that is, money used to finance a government deficit. The definition is directly applicable to later policy analysis.

In summary, one may relate domestically financed government borrowing to the following variables: reserve requirements, Central Bank discount policy, asset structure, policy of financial institutions, and the compulsory discount tool. A change in any of these will influence high-powered money. Therefore, in the short run the Central Bank may increase domestically financed foreign borrowing, thereby lowering the change in domestic credit and ultimately reducing high-powered money. Domestic government borrowing and the money supply are negatively related. On the other hand, liquidation of debt or purchase of outstanding notes by the Mexican government will be positively related to the money supply. One concludes, therefore, that the Mexican Central Bank has available to it tools similar to those of the U.S. Federal Reserve System to adjust the money stock in the short run through i_b. To the extent that the use of these tools by monetary authorities is not offset by nongovernment foreign borrowing, the employment of these controls will effect a change in H.*

To the extent that taxes and borrowing do not offset government expenditures (Y_g), the rate of government expenditures is also a factor in determining domestic credit. Although the government may clearly use Y_g as a control factor for creation of high-powered money, its importance as a policy instrument is not analyzed here except for the obvious: any increase in government expenditures will have to be offset by taxes or domestic borrowing. Otherwise, domestic credit will increase, in that all Y_g exceeding $(i_b + t)$ must be met by the Central Bank's creating money (domestic credit) required to fill the gap.

Foreign reserves work through high-powered money to change the money supply. As indicated earlier, changing gR or ΔD will create movements in H that can effect a change in the money supply through the multiplier process. The value of using this alternative specification for ΔD lies in its applicability to policy analysis, since ΔD can be set along with the fiscal policy variables Y_g, i_b, and t.

Setting money demand equal to the specified money supply equation, one may generate a reserve flow equation for Mexico. This equation will incorporate the information provided by the alternative approach to domestic credit, the money multiplier in component form, and the specified money demand equation.

---

*It should be observed that the Mexican government is actively promoting private borrowing. The process is carried out by the Central Bank's actively providing incentives to private banks and *financieras* to gain foreign deposits. One incentive is in the form of curtailing liquidity for the private sector while simultaneously providing a fiscal climate for increased private investment. Other legislative acts have provided a climate in which investor interests are protected through a set of tax incentives, guarantees on deposits, and complete banker-client discretion.

Reserve Flow Model

The basic theoretical model for the monetary approach to the balance of payments is outlined by Zecher. Following this general approach, we are able to specify the following model and derive reduced form equations.

$$M^S = a \cdot H \tag{25}$$

$$a = \frac{1 + K}{r + K} \tag{26}$$

where $r = r^d + e$

$$H = R + D$$

$$\frac{M^d}{P} = \frac{y^{a_1} e}{i^{a_2}} \tag{26a}$$

where e is a log-normally distributed error term.

$$M^S = M^d \tag{26b}$$

and the money demand can be rewritten as

$$M^d = \frac{P^{\beta_1} y^{a_1} e}{i^{a_2}} \tag{27}$$

given the assumption that money demand is linearly homogeneous in prices. Since

$$M^S = a \cdot (R + D) \quad \text{and} \quad M^S = M^d \tag{27a}$$

then

$$a \cdot (R + D) = \frac{P^{\beta_1} y^{a_1} e}{i^{a_2}} \tag{27b}$$

Taking percentage changes with respect to time and defining $gx = (dx/dt)(1/x)$,

$$ga + (R/H)gR + (D/H)gD = \beta_1 gP + a_1 gy - a_2 gi + e \tag{27c}$$

Defining $(R/H)gR$ as the dependent variable,

$$(R/H)gR = a_1 gy - a_2 gi + \beta_1 gP - ga - (D/H)gD + e \tag{27d}$$

A priori it is anticipated that

$$a_1 = +1, \quad a_2 < 0, \quad \text{and} \quad \beta_1 > 1$$

Alternatively, one could further expand the model by the following:
Since

$$a = \frac{1 + K}{r + K}$$

then

$$\frac{1 + K}{r + K} \cdot (R + D) = \frac{y^{a_1} P^{\beta_1} e}{i^{a_2}} \tag{28}$$

Taking logs to the base e,

$$\ln \left(\frac{1 + K}{r + K} \right) + \ln (R + D) = a_1 \ln y - a_2 \ln i + \beta_1 \ln P + \ln e \tag{28a}$$

Taking derivatives with respect to time,

$$gK \left(\frac{Kr - K}{K^2 + Kr + K + r} \right) - gr \left(\frac{r}{r + K} \right) + (R/H)gR + (D/H)gD$$

$$= \beta_1 gP + a_1 gy - a_2 gi + e' \tag{28b}$$

Following equation (27),

$$(R/H)gR = a_1 gy - a_2 gi + \beta_1 gP - gK \left(\frac{Kr - K}{K^2 + Kr + K + r} \right)$$

$$+ gr \left(\frac{r}{r + K} \right) - (D/H)gD + e \tag{29}$$

Equation (29) differs from equation (27d) in two terms as a result of the respecification of the money multiplier to its base components. Further specification of the monetary approach to the balance of payments should utilize the identity of $\Delta D \equiv Y_g - t - i_b$. Incorporating this new information into equation (27d), one obtains

$$\left(\frac{R}{H} \right) gR = a_1 gy - a_2 gi + \beta_1 gP - ga - \left(\frac{D}{H} \right) \left(\frac{Y_g}{D} - \frac{t}{D} - \frac{i_b}{D} \right) + e \tag{30}$$

Equation (30) may be restated as

$$\left(\frac{R}{H}\right)gR = a_1\,gy - a_2\,gi + \beta_1\,gP - ga - \frac{Y_g}{H} + \frac{t}{H} + \frac{i_b}{H} + e \tag{31}$$

Equation (31) represents the specification of the monetary model where domestic credit is broken into its base components.

An increase in government expenditures will imply an outflow of reserves, while an increase in either taxes or government debt issue would be positively related to reserves. Again Y_g is negatively related to $gR(R/H)$. The positive relation of $(R/H)gR$ to i_b is clear. An increase in government foreign borrowing necessarily increases foreign reserves, while an increase in domestic borrowing will have a positive effect on foreign reserves through two channels. First, domestic borrowing lowers the need to finance government expenditure through money creation. Second, an increase in domestic borrowing decreases the liquidity available for the private sector. In Mexico the policy of the government has been to promote foreign borrowing by private investors, thus increasing the reserve level in response to a tightening of credit available from domestically created resources. In discussion with officials at the Banco de México, this analyst was told that the increased government borrowing since 1971 has forced many private investors to seek foreign loans that would not otherwise have been pursued.

It is clear that the signs of the variables are negative for Y_g/H and positive for t/H and i_b/H. Incorporating the information concerning the specifications of domestic credit into equation (29), one obtains

$$\left(\frac{R}{H}\right)gR = a_1\,gy - a_2\,gi + \beta_1\,gP - gK\left(\frac{Kr - K}{K^2 + Kr + K + r}\right)$$
$$+ gr\left(\frac{r}{r + K}\right) - \frac{Y_g}{H} + \frac{t}{H} + \frac{i_b}{H} + e \tag{32}$$

This final specification breaks down both domestic credit and the money multiplier into component parts. Again, one can predict that the signs of a_2, $gK\left(\dfrac{Kr - K}{K^2 + Kr + K + r}\right)$ and Y_g/H will be negative. The signs of a_1, β_1, $gr\left(\dfrac{r}{r + K}\right)$, t/H, and i_b/H are expected to be positive.*

---

*Since $(dD/dt) = Y_g - i_b - t$, one may integrate the expression with respect to time as follows:

$$D = \int_{t_0}^{t_p} Y_g\,dt - \int_{t_0}^{t_p} i_b\,dt - \int_{t_0}^{t_p} t\,dt$$

That is, domestic credit is the total government expenditure from t_0 to t_p minus total government borrowing from t_0 to t_p minus total fiscal receipts from t_0 to t_p. D is additively related to these variables.

SUMMARY

In this chapter we have specified several variations of the monetary approach reduced form equations. The expansion of the model to incorporate the fiscal policy variables in equation (31) permits attention to be placed upon the policy alternatives available to the authorities. Since the creation of domestic credit is left over from determination of other policy variables—Y_g, t, and i_b—it can be interpreted as one possible variable in a mix (Y_g, t, i_b, and ΔD) of different policy alternatives. It may be more important to analyze these other variables while concentrating on domestic credit creation as a residual portion of the overall matrix of policy variables.

Further, it is useful to examine theoretically the components of the money multiplier; in subsequent chapters we analyze the movements of these components over time. However, the actual estimation of the parameters of the component variables yields little new information about the stability of the monetary approach relationship. Thus, as we turn to the empirical examination of our model, attention is directed to the behavioral relationships that are most useful for policy applications. First, we search for empirical support of the price and interest rate assumption. Second, the money demand relationship is examined. Finally, we examine the reduced forms of the monetary approach model.

NOTES

1. B. Griffiths, *Mexican Monetary Policy and Economic Development* (New York: Praeger, 1972), p. 4.

2. See Benjamin Higgins, *Economic Development: Problems, Principles, and Policies* (New York: Norton, 1968), p. 281.

3. Gilberto Escobedo, "Mexican Stabilization Policy, Fiscal or Monetary?," working paper, Bank of Mexico, 1973, p. 4.

4. See Gilberto Escobedo, "The Response of the Mexican Economy to Policy Action," *Federal Reserve of St. Louis Review* 55 (June 1973): 15–23.

5. See M. Friedman and D. Meiselman, "The Relative Stability of Monetary Velocity and the Investment Multiplier in the U.S. 1897–1958," in *Commission on Money and Credit, Stabilization Policies* (Englewood Cliffs, N.J.: Prentice-Hall, 1973), pp. 165–268. See also Albert Burger, *The Money Supply Process* (Belmont, Calif.: Wadsworth, 1971). For more in-depth discussion of the advantages and disadvantages of defining money as M_1 or M_2 in Mexico, see Gilberto Escobedo, "Los indicadores para medir el resultado de la política monetaria en México," *Comercio exterior* 23 (October 1973): 1007–15.

6. Gilberto Escobedo, "Mexican Stabilization Policy, Fiscal or Monetary?," pp. 13–16.

7. Harry Johnson, *Further Essays in Monetary Economics* (Cambridge, Mass.: Harvard University Press, 1973), p. 231.

8. See Jacob Viner, *Studies in the Theory of International Trade* (New York: Harper, 1927); F. W. Taussig, *International Trade* (New York: Macmillan, 1927); Joan Robinson, "The Foreign Exchange," in American Economic Association, *Readings in the Theory of International Trade* (Homewood, Ill.: Richard D. Irwin, 1950), pp. 23–103.

9. See J. E. Meade, *The Balance of Payments* (London: Oxford University Press, 1951); R. Mundell, *International Economics* (New York: Macmillan, 1968), ch. 16; and J. J. Polak, "Monetary Analysis of Income Formation and Payments Problems," *IMF Staff Paper* (November 1957).

10. See Johnson, op. cit.; J. Frenkel and C. Rodríguez, "Portfolio Equilibrium and the Balance of Payments: A Monetary Approach," *American Economic Review* 65 (September 1975): 674–78; A. B. Laffer, "Monetary Policy and the Balance of Payments," *Journal of Money, Credit, and Banking* 4 (February 1972): 13–22; M. G. Porter, "The Interdependence of Monetary Policy and Capital Flows in Australia," *Economic Record* 24 (August 1974): 120–50; M. G. Porter and R. J. Kouri, "International Capital Flows and Portfolio Equilibrium," *Journal of Political Economy* 82 (August 1974); Richard Zecher, "Monetary Equilibrium and International Reserve Flows in Australia," *Journal of Finance* 29 (December 1974): 1323–30; Bijan B. Aghevli and Mohsin S. Khan, "The Monetary Approach to the Balance of Payments Determination: An Empirical Test," paper presented at the American Economic Association convention, San Francisco, December 1974; John Rutledge, "Balance of Payments and Money Demand," paper presented at the Southern Economic Association meetings, New Orleans, November 1975; H. Genberg, Chapter 13 in J. Frenkel and H. G. Johnson, *The Monetary Approach to the Balance of Payments* (London: Allan and Unwin, 1976); and A. K. Swoboda, "Monetary Policy Under Fixed Exchange Rates: Effectiveness, the Speed of Adjustment and Proper Use," *Economica* 40, 100–58.

11. Johnson, op. cit., p. 237.

12. Aghevli and Khan, op. cit., pp. 1–10.

13. Johnson, loc. cit.

14. A. K. Swoboda, "Monetary Approaches to Balance-of-Payments Theory," in Karl Brunner and Starky Fischer, eds., *Recent Issues in International Monetary Economics* (New York: North-Holland, 1976), pp. 2–23.

15. Johnson, op. cit., pp. 229–49; Zecher, loc. cit.; Aghevli and Khan, op. cit., pp. 1–12; John Deavers, "The Chilean Inflation and the Demand for Money," in David M. Meiselman, ed., *Varieties of Monetary Experience* (Chicago: University of Chicago Press, 1970), pp. 7–67; Philip Cagan, *Determinants and Effects of Changes in the Stock of Money, 1875–1960* (New York: National Bureau of Economic Research, 1965); Karl Brunner and Allan H. Meltzer, "Predicting Velocity: Implications for Theory and Policy," *Journal of Finance* 18 (May 1963): 319–54; and Milton Friedman, "The Demand for Money: Some Theoretical and Empirical Results," *Journal of Political Economy* 67 (August 1959): 327; and "Interest Rates and the Demand for Money," *Journal of Law and Economics* 9 (October 1966): 72. For a recent study see W. Michael Cox, "Rational Expectations, the Monetary Approach to the Balance of Payments, and the Role of Monetary Policy in the Open Economy," mimeographed working paper, 1976.

16. Philip Cagan, "The Monetary Dynamics of Hyperinflation," in Milton Friedman, ed., *Studies in the Quantity Theory of Money* (Chicago: University of Chicago Press, 1956), pp. 25–117.

17. Milton Friedman, "The Quantity Theory of Money–A Restatement," ibid., pp. 3–24.

18. Deavers, op. cit., p. 23.

19. Milton Friedman, ed., "The Optimal Quantity of Money," in his *The Optimum Quantity of Money and Other Essays* (Chicago: Aldine, 1969), pp. 1–50.

20. See D. S. Wilford, "The Demand for Foreign Reserves in Mexico," unpublished master's thesis, Vanderbilt University, 1973; W. T. Wilford and J. M. Villaususo, "Central America: The Demand for Money in the Common Market," *Economic and Social Studies* 24 (June 1975): 209–220; A. Monte Mayor, "La demanda de dinero: El caso de México," unpublished thesis, Faculty of Economics, University of Nuevo León, 1969.

21. John Rutledge, *A Monetarist Model of Inflationary Expectations* (Lexington, Mass.: D. C. Heath, 1974).

22. For a more detailed discussion of the econometric specification equation (15), see ibid., chs. 3 and 4.

23. See Frank Zahn, *Macroeconomic Theory and Policy* (Englewood Cliffs, N.J.: Prentice-Hall, 1975), pp. 78–94.

24. In the presentation of the money supply process in Mexico, notation will follow, where possible, that of Albert Burger, *The Money Supply Process* (Belmont, Calif.: Wadsworth, 1971).

25. G. H. Borts and J. A. Hanson, "The Monetary Approach to the Balance of Payments," Unpublished working paper, Brown University, 1975.

3

THE MONETARY APPROACH TO
THE BALANCE OF PAYMENTS:
EMPIRICAL RESULTS

This chapter reports the empirical results of the analysis. First, the assumptions of price and interest rate determination are analyzed. Second, we examine both the real and the nominal demand for money in Mexico. Third, we scrutinize the results of the monetary approach to the balance-of-payments equation for Mexico. Finally, we utilize quarterly data to further examine the money demand and monetary models.

PRICE LEVELS AND INTEREST RATE ARBITRAGE

As noted in the development of the theoretical models, the monetary approach to the balance of payments treats prices and interest rates as exogenous variables because they are determined by the world marketplace. The Mexican rate of interest and price level should be equal to the world rate of interest and price level, respectively. This derives from the view that the world is a closed economy made up of many smaller open economies. The world is, therefore, a unified market for goods and assets. Then, under the condition of a fixed exchange rate, prices and rates of return on assets (or the interest rate) of different countries must move very closely. Integration of an individual country's goods market can be empirically examined through intercountry price

Some of the following discussion on prices and interest rates appeared in a previously published article. See D. S. Wilford, "Price Levels, Interest Rate, Open Economies and a Fixed Exchange Rate: The Mexican Case, 1954–1974," *Review of Business and Economic Research*, 12 (Spring 1977).

comparison. The integration of the assets market can be verified by examining intercountry interest rate levels.

Price Levels

If countries are closely tied together in the goods and services markets, then international arbitrage, expectation of arbitrage possibilities, or the assumption of full information would ensure that the prices of each country would move very closely. That is, either ability to arbitrage out any differential in prices that might exist, or simply the expectation of arbitrage possibilities becoming available, will ensure that prices move together. The assumption of full information concerning world prices will enable persons to disallow existence of any arbitrage possibilities. Individual goods could have different price levels due to tariffs, quotas, subsidies, or other factors. However, given that there are not substantial changes in these factors, one would anticipate that the changes in general prices would be very similar. Therefore, to examine the assumption of a unified goods market, one may examine the inflation rate of Mexico as it relates to the world rate of inflation. Since the United States is the largest trading partner of Mexico, borders Mexico (which reduces transportation costs), and is the leading foreign capital market for Mexico, the U.S. price index is used as a proxy for the world rate.

The hypothesis of a unified goods market requires that the rate of inflation in Mexico be close to the rate of inflation in the United States. However, divergences could occur, since different market baskets are used to determine these rates. One may test the unified goods market hypothesis by examining Mexico's rate of inflation as it relates to the U.S. rate of inflation.

Formally,

$$\pi_m = \pi_{us} + u$$

where π_m = Mexican inflation rate
π_{us} = United States inflation rate
u   = random disturbance caused by differences in the methods of calculating the consumer price index and other factors.

If the rates of inflation for Mexico and the United States were different, then one model could be stated as

$$\pi_m = \pi_{us} + \beta_m + u \tag{33}$$

where β_m = the difference in Mexican and U.S. rates of inflation.

TABLE 3.1

Regression of Inflation Rates in Mexico on Inflation Rates in the United States, Various Periods

$$(\pi_m = \beta_0 + \beta_1 \pi_{us} + u)$$

	Period			
	195902–197404	195902–197004	196501–197004	196501–197404
Equation number	1	2	3	4
Constant	0.301	0.322	0.763	0.335
	(1.739)	(1.440)	(2.293)	(1.300)
β_1	0.926	0.628	0.198	0.921
	(9.127)	(2.322)	(0.719)	(7.548)
R^2	.520	.15	.283	.540
F-value	64.48	8.01	8.289	43.030
DW	1.898	1.966	2.297	1.763
RHO	0.366 (1)	.140	−0.05	0.391 (1)
	−0.538 (2)			−0.622 (2)

Notes: Quarterly percentage changes are used.

The t-statistics are in parentheses under their respective coefficients.

Source: Compiled by the author.

A measure of the degree to which the Mexican rates of inflation depend upon the world rates would be a hint of the measure of the functional relationship of Mexican rates and world rates. Referring to equation (33), the relationship of the Mexican rate to the U.S. rate is

$$\pi_m = \beta_0 + \beta_1 \pi_{us} + u \qquad (34)$$

β_0 is expected to be 0 if the countries are closely integrated, and we anticipate that the value of β_1 is close to 1. Table 3.1 presents the results for different periods, using quarterly data.

The results show that over the entire period 1959–74 the Mexican and the U.S. inflation rates were approximately the same. The coefficient for regression 1 of β_0 is insignificant at $a = .05$, while the coefficient of β_1 is significantly different from 0 but not from its hypothesized value 1. The F-value is high and $R^2 = .52$, indicating that much of the variation has not been captured.

The subperiod 1965–74 also yields good results. The hypothesis that $\beta_0 = 0$ and $\beta_1 = 1$ cannot be rejected at $a = .05$. The F-level is high and the R^2 acceptable. The results of the 1959–70 subperiod are good, with both an insignificant constant and β_1 not significantly different from 1. Mexico's rate of inflation over the period appears to have followed the world rate. For 1965–70 the constant is significant and the confidence interval of β_1 ($a = .05$) contains 0, because we have a standard error of $\hat\beta_1$ of .275 and $\hat\beta_1 = .198$; however, casually, this period appears to be the most stable, since the consumer price indexes of Mexico and the United States moved very closely.

An investigation of annual data for the period 1954–73 yields interesting results. From estimating equation (34) we obtain the results

$$\pi_m = 4.462 + 0.212\,\pi_{us} \qquad\qquad R^2 = .01$$
$$(2.904)\ (0.438) \qquad\qquad\qquad\qquad F = .192$$
$$DW = 1.608$$

The regression shows that the U.S. inflation rate is insignificant in explaining the rate of inflation in Mexico. Also, the $\hat\beta_0 > 0$ is significant. The results of the equation are dubious because the $R^2 = .01$ and the F-value is insignificant.

However, if we exclude observations for 1954 and 1955, on the grounds that the devaluation took place in 1954 and adjustment would possibly be taking place through 1955, then for 1956–73

$$\pi_m = 1.747 + 0.9280\,\pi_{us} \qquad\qquad R^2 = .282$$
$$(1.414)\ (2.509) \qquad\qquad\qquad\qquad F = 6.298$$
$$DW = 1.238$$

These results are as would be predicted by the unified goods market hypothesis. The coefficient $\hat\beta_0$ is not significantly different from 0 and $\hat\beta_1$ is significant and close to 1.

Both quarterly and annual results indicate that the Mexican price level is a proxy for the world levels. The evidence suggests that for a country such as Mexico, the rate of inflation will be exogenously determined under a fixed exchange rate system.

As was the case following the two previous devaluations in Mexico, rapid inflation occurred after 1954. In 1955 the rate was 15 percent, although in 1953 the rate had shown slight negative growth. Though the consumer price index was 62.7 in 1954 (1967 = 100), compared with the U.S. index of 87.70 (1967 = 100), by 1956 the gap had closed to only 12 points. In 1960 they had equilibrated. The rates of change for the United States and Mexico showed substantial variation only during 1954 and 1955, precisely the period in which the disturbance created by devaluation occurred. This fact is confirmed by our empirical results, which indicate that in the long run the price indexes in Mexico and the United States move together.

Interest Rates

Examination of the nominal interest rate in Mexico vis-a-vis the U.S. rate indicates the extent to which the bond markets are related. Figures 3.1 and 3.2 show the time path of nominal composite interest rates for both Mexico and the United States. It is interesting to note that Mexican interest rates are stable in comparison with those of the United States. For example, long-term Mexican rates showed only a slight decline between 1965 and 1970, while those in the United States increased sharply over the period. This apparent contradiction of the unified capital hypothesis will be clarified by examining the change in the relative liquidity preference of Mexican borrowers.

One may test the hypothesis that the Mexican rate of interest is a proxy for the world rate on the basis of the two data series. Let $i_m = F(i_w)$ where i_m = the Mexican rate of interest. Let i_w = the world rate of interest; that is,

FIGURE 3.1

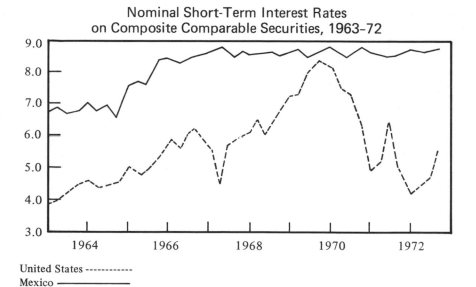

Nominal Short-Term Interest Rates
on Composite Comparable Securities, 1963–72

United States -----------
Mexico ————————

Source: Compiled by the author.

FIGURE 3.2

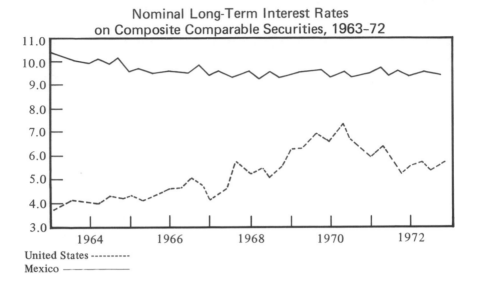

Nominal Long-Term Interest Rates
on Composite Comparable Securities, 1963–72

United States ----------
Mexico ——————

Source: Compiled by the author.

the Mexican rate is determined by the world rate. The functional form is

$$i_m = \theta + \beta i_w + e \qquad (35)$$

where

      θ = constant
      e = normally distributed error term

One would expect θ to be relatively large for countries that have political instability, a history of devaluation, less financial stability, and so forth. The coefficient θ is a measure, to some extent, of a premium above the world rate paid by
Mexico for funds.

    One should also investigate the relative movements of interest rates. Such
movements should be free of the θ term in equation (35). The relationship in a
linear form is

$$gi_m = \beta_0 + \beta_1 gi_w + e' \qquad (36)$$

where

gi_m = percentage change in i_m
gi_w = percentage change in i_w
e' = a stochastic disturbance term

The term β_0 is anticipated to take the value of 0, since any constant differential due to liquidity premium would be eliminated. If $\beta_0 = 0$, the value of β_1 should be positive.*

To test the hypothesis that there are interest rate differentials, one may examine equation (35). If a mean differential exists, β_0 will differ from 0. Alternatively, one may wish to see if the growth rates of the interest rates differ; and to test this hypothesis, equation (36) is examined. If the growth rates differ, $\beta_0 \neq 0$. A test of these two hypotheses may be made with analysis of variance (ANOVA) techniques. The results of these tests are reported for Belgium, France, Germany, Netherlands, Canada, and Mexico. In these tests, the United States is considered as the rest of the world. Table 3.2 reports the test results for short-term rates in 1960–72, using quarterly data. Short-term rates show $\theta \neq 0$ ($a = .05$) for Belgium, France, Netherlands, and Mexico. Germany and Canada exhibited no average differential for the period. Mexico registered the strongest F (75.48), while Germany showed the lowest (0.324). The table further shows that growth rates for each country, except Mexico, were approximately the same, $\beta_0 = 0$. For Mexico this test suggests that the average change in short-term rates there is different from that in the United States.

Table 3.3 presents results for long-term rates using quarterly data covering 1960–72. The average long-term rate for each country appears to differ from the U.S. rate. Mexico has the highest F-level (1,135.0), and $\theta = 0$ can be rejected for all countries tested. Examination of the average growth rates shows no case of $\beta_0 \neq 0$. The hypothesis that mean growth rates differ significantly is rejected for each country. These results suggest that Mexican long-term rates react predictably, according to the unified capital market hypothesis. That is, i_m is a positive function of i_w and the mean gi_m does not differ significantly from mean gi_w for 1960–72.

A further test of the hypothesis that Mexican interest rates are a proxy for world rates may be undertaken by utilizing regression analysis to examine the movements of interest rates over time. Mexico is clearly a developing economy. During the 1950s and 1960s it rapidly expanded the services of its financial sector. The amount of premium required to discount Mexican notes vis-a-vis the United States may vary. For example, as Mexico grows more politically,

---

*Equation (36) can be derived from the relationship $i_m = e^{\beta_0} i_w^{\beta_1}$. If $\beta_0 = 0$, then $e^{\beta_0} = 1$; therefore $i_m = i_w^{\beta_1}$. Then $\beta_1 > 0$.

TABLE 3.2

ANOVA Test on U.S. Short-Term Interest Rates, 1960–72 (quarterly data)

Country	i	Percent Δi	F-Value	Probability
Belgium	X		14.690	0.0002
Belgium		X	0.083	0.7135
France	X		11.060	0.0012
France		X	1.581	0.2112
Germany[a]	X		0.324	0.5700
Germany		X	1.653	0.2011
Netherlands	X		10.070	0.0019
Netherlands		X	0.046	0.8309
Canada[a]	X		0.403	0.5265
Canada		X	0.056	0.8131
Mexico	X		75.480	0.0000
Mexico[b]		X	10.080	0.0020

[a]The mean rates of interest are very close, not significantly different from 0 at the .05 level.

[b]Mexico is the only country that shows the mean percentage change in i different from that in the United States.

Sources: Informe Anual 1973 (Mexico City: Bank of Mexico, 1974); *International Financial Statistics* (Washington, D.C.: International Monetary Fund), *Statistics on the Mexican Economy*, and the Bank of Mexico.

economically, and financially stable, the premium will fall. In short, the trend in Mexican rates will decline with respect to the United States as a result of the increased relative desirability of the Mexican peso.

First we employ regression analysis to examine the movements over the period of the study in Mexican, relative to American, interest rates. Just as regression analysis was employed on the goods market by examining percentage changes in the price level, it is possible to test the hypothesis that the percentage changes in the interest rate yield a similar relationship. Specifying a regression model

$$gi_m = \theta + \beta gi_{us} + u \tag{37}$$

where

u = an error term
θ = the constant

one may test for the values of θ and β. Annual results from 1951 through 1974 yielded

$$gi_m = 0.369 + 0.039\ gi_{us}$$
$$(0.344)\ (0.854)$$

$R^2 = .031$
$F = 0.699$
$DW = 2.17$

Similar results were obtained for the 1954-74 period:

$$gi_m = 0.019 + 0.124\ gi_{us}$$
$$(0.142)\ (0.133)$$

$R^2 = .001$
$F = .018$
$DW = 2.26$

These regressions both have insignificant F-levels, low R^2s, and insignificant t-statistics on the coefficients. The results provide little evidence to suggest that the growth rates of the Mexican interest rate are significantly related to growth rates of the U.S. interest rate.

As the financial structure of the Mexican economy evolved over the period, the relation of the Mexican market rate of interest to the U.S. rate

TABLE 3.3

ANOVA Test on U.S. Long-Term Interest Rates, 1960-72
(quarterly data)

Country	i	Percent Δi	F-Value	Probability
Belgium	X		61.9100	0.0000
Belgium		X	0.3468	0.5571
France	X		36.8100	0.0000
France		X	0.2540	0.6151
Germany	X		119.1000	0.0000
Germany		X	0.1050	0.7458
Netherlands	X		14.9700	0.0020
Netherlands		X	0.0190	0.8880
Canada	X		41.2000	0.0000
Canada		X	0.1620	0.6875
Mexico	X		1135.0000	0.0000
Mexico		X	0.978	0.3252

Note: The F-levels indicate that the mean interest rate is significantly different at the .05 level for each country with respect to the United States, and that there is no significant difference in the average rate of changes in interest rates.

Sources: Informe Anual 1973 (Mexico City: Bank of Mexico, 1974); *International Financial Statistics* (Washington, D.C.: International Monetary Fund), *Statistics on the Mexican Economy*, and the Bank of Mexico.

also changed. The narrowing of rates could be observed empirically over time with the increased vitality of the Mexican financial sector. Time may be used as a proxy for the growth in political and economic stability in Mexico. The Mexican interest rate can be seen as a function of time, and the world rate of interest is also empirically related to time. An examination of Figures 3.1 and 3.2 suggests that Mexican rates may, however, be related to time differently than world rates are; and one method of analyzing this problem is to evaluate the movements around the trend for Mexican and U. S. rates. The factors that are not functions of time that operate on both the Mexican and the U. S. rates will then be taken into account. Therefore, one may examine these relationships by comparing the residual of a regression of the form

$$i_j = \beta_{0j} + \beta_{ij} T + u_j \tag{38}$$

where

i_j = the jth country's interest rate
T = time
u_j = the stochastic distribution term

Upon obtaining the estimated equation form $i_j = \beta_{0j} + \beta_{1j} T + e_j$, then e may be calculated by $e_j = i_j - \hat{i}_j$, where $i_j = \beta_0 + \beta_{ij} T$. Having calculated e_j for Mexico and the United States, one may compare these residuals.

Testing the hypothesis that the e_m and e_{us} (Mexican and U.S. residuals, respectively) are related should indicate the degree to which the world interest rate is reflected in the reported Mexican interest rates. Since the growth in the financial community of Mexico vis-a-vis the United States is now considered in equation (38), one can expect the variation in the residuals to be affected by the variations in the world interest rate around its trend. The theoretical form of the equation is

$$e_m = \beta_1 + \beta_2 e_{us} + u \tag{39}$$

where u = the stochastic distribution term. The estimated equation form is

$$e_m = b_0 + b_1 e_{us} + e \tag{40}$$

where b_0 and b_1 are estimated values of β_1 and β_2, respectively. The results of equations (38) and (39) are reported in Tables 3.4 and 3.5. Table 3.4 presents the results for long-term interest rates, and Table 3.5 presents the results for short-term interest rates. In both cases the regressions were for quarterly data for the stated period.*

The results of the regression for both Mexico and the United States (where the trend was eliminated and e was calculated) were acceptable. The F-levels are all acceptable and R^2s are high. However, examination of regression 3 and 6 for both tables indicates that the residuals are not systematically related. The F-levels are all insignificant and R^2s very low. The t-statistics on b_1 for both long-term and short-term interest rates are all insignificant. We thus conclude that for the period 1960–72 and for the subperiod 1965–72 there appears to be very little relation between e_m and e_{us}.

Though these results provide little support for the theory of unified capital markets, they are not unexpected. The actual market rate of interest reported is controlled since there is no significant secondary bond market. Clark Reynolds suggests that the aim of the government has been to tie the loan rate of interest to the discount rate and, by fixing it at a level below the equilibrium market rate, has been able to ration credit. Though Reynolds sees this as a second-best solution, he suggests that it may be important in improving expectations of investors.[1]

Robert Bennett notes that the interest rates on "primary securities and indirect securities were usually held at fixed levels by the financial authorities."[2] R. W. Goldsmith says that one specific characteristic of the financial structure is "the prevalence among financial instruments of high coupon obligations of private and public institutions which are actually repayable on demand, although in form they often are of medium and long-term maturities."[3]

Fixed-interest securities are the issues most traded on the Mexican securities markets, but are traded to and from the issuer. The fixed-interest bonds are such that one can receive payment upon demand, if desired. This type of issue is important in the maintenance of public confidence in an assured return on savings, but the result is that secondary markets, where legal, are mostly eliminated.

Since the rate of interest either is set by the government authorities or, as in the bond market, is fixed by the nature of the market, the reported nominal rate of interest is not a true market rate. As a result of government decision to keep the private loan rate below the equilibrium rate, the government is better able to control credit allocation from domestic sources. This arrangement can lead to nonoptimal allocation of resources, as Reynolds suggests. More important, however, is that the differential between the actual market rate and

---

*The data available to the author from the Central Bank of Mexico were better for the 1965–72 period than for the entire period, 1960–72.

TABLE 3.4

Long-Term Interest Rate Determination,
United States and Mexico, 1960–72

$$i_j = \beta_{0j} + \beta_{ij}T + u_j$$
$$e_m = \beta_1 + \beta_2 e_{us} + u$$

Period	Equation Number	Type of Rate	β_0	β_1	b_0	b_1	R^2	F	DW	RHO
1960–72	1	United States	4.09 (5.490)	0.006 (0.461)			.89	405	1.40	.907
1960–72	2	Mexico	6.432 (7.154)	0.004 (0.744)				2,305	1.88	.984
1960*–72	3				0.050 (1.990)	−0.021 (−0.418)	.004	0.175	2.04	—
1965–72	4	United States	3.931 (2.246)	0.026 (0.563)			.82	140.7	1.386	.825
1965–72	5	Mexico	6.577 (45.33)				.99	1,106.5	2.201	.710
1965–72	6				0.010 (0.814)	0.007 (0.346)	.004	0.120	2.268	—

*Regression period 1960, second quarter; 1972, fourth quarter.
Source: Compiled by the author.

TABLE 3.5

Short-Term Interest Rate Determination, United States and Mexico, 1960–72

$$(I_j = \beta_{0j} + \beta_{ij}T + u_j)$$
$$(e_m = \beta_1 + \beta_2 e_{us} + u)$$

Period	Equation Number	Type of Rate	β_0	β_1	b_0	b_1	R^2	F	DW	RHO
1960–72	1	United States	4.808 (7.720)	.0031 (0.4969)			.97	1,642	1.60	.97
1960–72	2	Mexico	9.571 (43.808)	-0.001 (-0.117)			.99	5,503	1.97	.91
1960*–72	3				0.0255 (0.930)	-0.202 (-0.954)	.018	.911	1.67	—
1965–72	4	United States	3.321 (3.604)	0.052 (2.199)			.96	831.4	1.52	.89
1965–72	5	Mexico	9.729 (48.48)	-0.007 (-1.356)			.99	11,637	2.24	.75
1965–72	6				-0.009 (-0.626)	0.027 (0.402)	.005	.162	2.210	—

*Regression period 1960, second quarter; 1972, fourth quarter.
Source: Compiled by the author.

the official rates will lead to alternative forms of credit allocation by investors and lenders.

The conclusion from our study can only be that the reported rates of interest for Mexico are not market rates. This suggests that the results obtained in Tables 3.4 and 3.5 are difficult to interpret. Further, the results of the tests cannot be considered evidence that the capital markets of the United States and Mexico are segmented. While some doubt is cast upon the validity of using the reported Mexican rates of interest as a proxy of world rates of interest, there is insufficient evidence to suggest that market rates for Mexico are not exogenously determined by the world rate of interest. But there is doubt about the validity of the reported interest rates for Mexico, since the limited-traded bond market does not permit a secondary market for fixed-interest securities. Further, reported nominal rates do not include all premiums paid to lending institutions for funds. For these reasons there is insufficient evidence to support any hypothesis that market rates for Mexico are not exogenously determined. The empirical results can, therefore, neither confirm nor deny the hypothesis of a unified capital market.

MONEY DEMAND

We may utilize the theoretical apparatus outlined in Chapter 2 to analyze demand for money in Mexico. Long-run determinants of money demand are identified by utilizing annual data.

The estimating equations for the real money demand equation and the nominal money demand equation are reported below. The real money demand estimation form is

$$g(M_1/P) = a_1 gy - a_2 gi + e \tag{41}$$

where

$$g(M_1/P) = \text{the growth rate of real money balances}$$
$$e = \text{a log normally distributed stochastic disturbance term}$$

The nominal money demand estimation form is

$$gM_1 = a_1 gy - a_2 gi + \beta_1 gP + e \tag{42}$$

where

$$gM_1 = \text{the growth rate of nominal money balances}$$

The data are annual for 1954–74 and are defined as follows:

y = real income of Mexico
i = long-term interest rate
P = consumer price index for Mexico
M_1 = nominal money supply: coins and currency in circulation plus
     demand deposits

We anticipate both a_1 and β_1 to take the value of +1. The sign of a_2 in this model is predicted to be negative, showing that an increase in the interest rate should lead to a decrease in the stock of money held in the portfolio.

The interpretation of the assumption of linear homogeneity of money with respect to prices is that people will adjust nominal money balance in proportion to the increases in the price level. Both the expected β_1 and the a_2 coefficients are, in part, based upon the small-country assumption. To the degree that real money demand is not related to income and the interest rate, the coefficients for the variables could differ from the anticipated values.

Table 3.6 reports regressions of estimating equations (41) and (42). Regressions 1 and 3 are for real money demand; regressions 2, 4, 5, and 6 are for nominal money demand. Regressions 1, 2, 3, and 4 use a Mexican long-term interest rate to serve for i, while regressions 5 and 6 use the U.S. rate of interest as a proxy of the world rate of interest.*

---

*The results should be interpreted in their most general form. In regressions 2 and 4 the β_1 coefficients are less than 1 though not significantly different at the 95 percent confidence level. This result could be interpreted as hinting that there exists money illusion as $\beta_1 < 1$. If interpreted in this manner, a better estimate of money demand is to constrain $\beta_1 = 1$. This would imply that perfect rationality exists with respect to prices and money. A reserve flow model that would utilize this assumption would incorporate the constraint into the model by constraining $\beta_1 = 1$ throughout. The result of testing this specific case where rationality in prices is explicitly assumed follows:

$$(R/H)Gr - gP = a_1\, gy - a_2\, gi - \beta_1\, ga - \beta_2\, gD(D/H) + \mu$$

where μ = a stochastic disturbance term. The results of testing this model for 1954–74 annual data are

$$(R/H)Gr - gP = \underset{(4.9107)}{.822gy} - \underset{(-1.476)}{0.295gi} - \underset{(-5.271)}{1.030ga} - \underset{(-8.661)}{1.034(D/H)gD}$$

R^2 = .866
F = 34.44
DW = 1.607

TABLE 3.6

Estimated Demand Equations for Money in Mexico, 1954–74

$$g(M_1/P) = a_1 gY + a_2 gi + e$$

$$g(M_1) = a_1 gY + a_2 gi + \beta_1 gP + e''$$

Period	Equation Number	Dependent Variable	Income Elasticity of Money Demand	Mexican Interest Rate Elasticity of Money Demand	U.S. Interest Rate Elasticity of Money Demand	β_1	R^2	F	RHO	DW
1954–70	1	$g(M_1/P)$	0.820 (2.202)	−0.296 (−1.309)			.41	4.44		1.64
1954–70	2	$g(M_1)$	0.893 (5.602)	−0.238 (−1.117)		0.857 (3.881)	.44	5.15	.139	1.99
1954–74	3	$g(M_1/P)$	1.010 (7.538)	−0.261 (1.356)			.38	10.81		1.66
1954–74	4	$g(M_1)$	0.989 (5.986)	−0.162 (−0.785)		0.837 (4.724)	.55	10.37	.180	1.88
1954–70	5	$g(M_1)$	1.024 (6.801)		−0.023 (−0.506)	0.758 (3.367)	.42	4.74		1.95
1954–74	6	$g(M_1)$	1.074 (6.613)		−0.032 (.702)	0.805 (4.710)	.31	4.03		1.82

Note: The t-statistics are reported in parentheses under the coefficient.
Source: Compiled by the author.

The results of the money demand regressions confirm expectations with respect to sign. However, the size of the coefficient for interest elasticity is small and in no case significantly ($a = .05$) different from 0. This is consistent with results of Richard Zecher and John Rutledge. The income elasticities and β_1 coefficients have the correct sizes and signs. All estimates of the coefficients for income elasticities and the β_1 are significant. The R^2 is low in all cases, but the F-levels are significant. The size of these R^2s indicates that much of the variation in real and nominal money balances for Mexico is not systematically related to changes in either income or the interest rate.

The assumption of money demand homogeneous of degree 1 in the price level cannot be rejected for any of the regressions. The hypothesis that $\beta_1 = 1$ is accepted. Therefore, the specifications of equations (23) and (42) are plausible with respect to prices.

The signs for the coefficients of the interest rate variable are consistent with the model though the significance is questionable. However, these results agree with other money demand studies for emerging nations. The substitution of the U. S. interest rate into the model yielded insignificant results, although the signs were correct. This test was made because the reported Mexican series of interest rates are questionable. The inclusion of U. S. rates did not improve the results (regression 5 and 6); the values are still far from unity and not significantly different from 0. These results agree with those of Antonio Gómez Oliver, who found the interest rate coefficient to be small in all cases and insignificant in most cases. Further, our real income elasticities agree with his study at approximate unity for M_1.[4]

In summary, the demand for real money in Mexico appears to be determined largely by real income, while the interest rate coefficient is not significant. The signs of the Mexican interest rate elasticity coefficients are as expected but are insignificant. This is not unanticipated, because of our earlier investigations of Mexican interest rate arbitrage. However, a similar result is obtained when the U. S. rate of interest is used as a proxy for the world rate. This again is plausible if one considers that much of the variation in the nominal interest rate is due to expectations of inflation. The inflation rate during this period has been relatively low, and therefore the relative costs of holding money vis-a-vis the adjustment costs apparently have not been large enough to induce strong responses in changes of money holdings to changes in the interest rate.

Nominal money demand responds proportionally to the price level, as anticipated. This is consistent with other money demand studies for Mexico and with the Zecher and Rutledge results. Our data confirm the hypothesis of linear homogeneity of money in prices.

ESTIMATED RESERVE FLOW MODEL

Referring to equation (27d), the reserve flow estimation equation has the form

$$(R/H)gR = a_1 gy - a_2 gi + \beta_1 gP - \beta_2 ga - \beta_3 (D/H)gD + u \qquad (43)$$

where

a = the money multiplier
R = foreign reserves
D = domestic credit
H = high-powered money
u = a stochastic disturbance term

The data are annual for the period 1954–74. The money multiplier, a, is calculated by dividing M_1 by H, while D is obtained from the identity $D \equiv H - R$.

It is anticipated that both a_1 and β_1 will take the value of +1. Coefficients β_2 and β_3 should take the value of –1. The sign of a_2 in this model is predicted to be negative, indicating that an increase in interest rates results in a net outflow of international reserves. The increase in the rate of interest would result in a decrease in the demand for money that is mirrored by a decrease in the demand for foreign reserves, ceteris paribus. Of course, if the domestic interest rate were allowed to differ from the world rate, then two forces would be at work with respect to reserves: a negative influence through the money demand function and a positive effect through the interest rate differential. In the monetary model the assumption of an open economy allows for free capital mobility and interest arbitrage; therefore the interest rate is assumed to be a proxy for the world rate of interest. The small-country assumption indicates that prices are exogenously determined. Therefore we expect that $\beta_1 = 1$ and that the price level in Mexico is a proxy for the world price level. Price changes will induce reserve inflows. An increase in the price level leads to a reduction in real money balance and thus, ceteris paribus, to a reserve inflow to maintain equilibrium.

One must note that the anticipated values depend upon the relation of money demand to income and the interest rate. To the degree that money demand is not related to income and the interest rate, the coefficients for all variables could differ from the anticipated values.

Estimation of equation (43) for 1954–74 yielded

$$(R/H)gR = 1.088gy - 0.079gi + 0.619gP - 1.071ga - 1.055(D/H)gD \qquad (44)$$
$$(6.238) \quad (-0.424) \quad (4.330) \quad (-6.457) \quad (-10.427)$$

The results are satisfactory and confirm our expectations. The value of a_1 is not significantly different from $+1$, while the value of β_1 is significantly different from 0 with the proper sign and the null hypothesis that $\beta_1 = 1$ cannot be rejected at the 99 percent level. The coefficient a_2 has the correct sign but is insignificant. Coefficients β_2 and β_3 have the expected sizes and signs, and are significant. Summary statistics are good; that is, the F-value is significant and the R^2 is high.

The results are similar to those of Zecher, Rutledge, B. J. Aghevli, and M. S. Kahn. The values of a_1, a_2, and β_1 are similar to the suggested results from the regressions in Table 3.6. The coefficients β_2 and β_3 are as predicted by the theoretical specification. The results indicate that a tight monetary policy, aimed at decreasing the money supply by lowering the growth rate of the money multiplier, will cause reserves to flow into Mexico in response. Similarly, the desire to tighten the domestic money supply by lowering domestic credit will stimulate revenue inflows. The size of the coefficients indicates that policy action will be fully offset by a resulting inflow of reserves.

In 1970 the monetary authorities were disturbed by an increasing rate of inflation. In response, they attempted to slow the growth in the money supply. That is, policy makers sought to maintain a growth rate in the money supply at a level approximating the growth rate in real income, as had been the policy during the 1950s and 1960s. Indeed, during 1954–70 this policy was easy to maintain. As the world money supply began to increase more rapidly in the late 1960s and early 1970s, and as prices began to rise, the ability of the Central Bank to carry out this policy was lessened. The monetary approach to the balance of payments explains that, as the price level increases, the demand for nominal money increases. In an effort to reduce the rate of inflation, the Central Bank used restrictive monetary policy during late 1970, 1971, and early 1972. It attempted to slow the rate of growth in the stock of money by lowering domestic credit and sharply reducing the money multiplier. The latter increased minimally in 1970, then fell by 5.23 percent in 1971 and by 29.53 percent in 1972. Domestic credit grew at a very low rate in 1970 and 1971 but finally accelerated in late 1972, and continued to grow in 1973 and 1974.

The attempt to control the money stock resulted in percentage increases in reserves of 12.39, 27.95, and 19.01 in 1970, 1971, and 1972, respectively, with a similar increase in 1973, and only a 2.72 percent increase in 1974. As the bank tried to slow money growth by restricting domestic resources, foreign reserves flowed inward at high levels during 1971, 1972, and 1973. While domestic credit was loosened in late 1972, 1973 and 1974, and the multiplier slowed its decline in 1974, the amount of foreign reserves needed to satisfy domestic demand began to level off. If during 1970, 1971, and 1972 the bank desired to maintain a slow growth in the money supply by using domestic controls, then according to the monetary approach to the balance of payments, foreign reserves

TABLE 3.7

Annualized Rates of Change in the Variables, 1955-74

Period	gR(R/H)	gy	(-)gi*	gP	(-)ga*	(-)gD(D/H)*
1955-60	0.03	5.91	0.00	6.76	1.80	7.42
1960-65	1.70	7.73	-0.15	1.93	1.52	7.50
1965-70	2.12	7.37	-0.89	3.98	-0.81	8.10
1970	3.49	6.14	-0.55	5.22	2.99	3.33
1971	7.76	2.17	0.00	5.74	-5.23	4.69
1972	3.93	7.78	-3.43	5.06	-29.53	37.94
1973	3.71	8.50	9.61	11.27	-4.94	19.73
1974	.75	6.01	5.17	22.00	-11.00	39.30

Note: The rates of change in R, y, i, p, a, and D have been averaged for the three five-year periods to compare with the four one-year periods.

*gi, ga, and gD carry negative influences on gR.

Source: Compiled by the author.

would flow inward to meet the excess demand for money. This was indeed the result of the policy actions.

The question of the validity of the monetary approach to the balance of payments during the period of economic disruption (1970-74) was raised earlier in the analysis, and the model was tested for the 1954-70 period of stability. The results were

$$(R/H)gR = 0.964gy - 0.105gi + 0.612gP - 0.624ga - 1.007(D/H)gD \quad (45)$$
$$(4.650) \quad (-0.465) \quad (2.855) \quad (-1.388) \quad (-8.675)$$

$R^2 = .92$
$F = 36.67$
$DW = 1.979$

These results of the reserve flow regression equation for the stable period are, on casual inspection, little different from those for the entire period (which included four years of economic disruption). The same result is also found in comparison of the demand-for-money regression equations, in which the shorter period again did not yield a better fit, nor did it give significantly different results. Neither the instability of the economy during this period nor the international crisis of the period appeared to affect the stability of the model. The only variable that seemed to be affected was ga. The coefficient of ga, -0.624 with a t-value of (-1.388), is insignificant and is absolutely (though not statistically) less than in the 1954-74 results. Indeed, the 1954-74 results appear to be better for β_2. The low t-statistic in the 1954-70 period may be due to the fact that there was very little movement in the money multiplier until 1970, when large variations were recorded. Indeed, results of the tests indicate that the monetary approach to the balance of payments performs well, especially given the economic disruptions during 1970-74.

Evaluation of the data is helpful in analyzing the reserve movements of the period. Table 3.7 compares annualized average growth rates for 1955-60, 1960-65, and 1965-70, along with the individual years 1970, 1971, 1972, 1973, and 1974. It permits one to analyze the forces operating on foreign reserve flows. The 1955-60 period recorded a 5.91 percent average real income growth rate. However, domestic credit expanded rapidly enough to satisfy money demand induced by real growth and a general price rise. The second period, 1960-65, shows a stronger growth in real income, although the price level did not increase appreciably. Therefore, a lower rate of increase in domestic credit could accommodate the demand for money. However, the slow growth rate of domestic credit, scaled by its contributions to high-powered money for the two periods, resulted in reserve inflow. The same pattern was followed during 1965-70, except that the multiplier movement reinforced inward flows of reserves.

The 1970s witnessed more erratic behavior. In 1970 a sizable inward flow of reserves occurred as domestic credit was tightened. This also held true in 1971, when the multiplier fell as a result of deliberate monetary policy of the Central Bank. Domestic credit was not allowed to grow rapidly. Finally, in 1972 domestic credit expanded rapidly. However, this expansion was coupled with a dramatic fall in the multiplier. Therefore the full effect, given the increase in real income and prices, was still an inflow of foreign reserves.

The year 1973 was similar except that domestic credit did not expand quite so rapidly as in 1972. Prices continued to increase more rapidly and again were reinforced by increases in real income. The combined effect caused inward flows in foreign reserves. The 1970, 1971, and 1972 policies of the Central Bank are reflected in the last two columns of Table 3.7. Tightening of credit in 1970, 1971, and early 1972 resulted not in a lower growth rate in the money stock but, rather, in inward flows of foreign reserves that were needed to satisfy the demand for money.

One may further investigate the model allowing money to be defined more broadly. Let money be composed of M_1 + various liquid assets in financial systems.* This broad definition yields the following results for equation (43) during 1954-72.

$$(R/H)gR = 1.126gy - 0.115gi + 0.776gP - 0.659ga - 1.007(D/H)gD \qquad (46)$$
$$(3.934) \quad (-0.511) \quad (3.032) \quad (-3.680) \quad (-6.734)$$

$$R^2 = .85$$
$$F = 18.73$$
$$DW = 1.45$$

Again, the results are as anticipated, with all coefficients having the correct size and sign. All coefficients except a_2 are significantly different from 0. This definition of money does not seriously affect the model. The F-level is significant and the R^2 high.

THE MONETARY APPROACH
AND BASIC EMPIRICAL RESULTS

The Mexican international reserve flows for 1954-74 are as would be predicted by the monetary approach to the balance of payments. The balance of

---

*This definition of M_2 follows Gilberto Escobedo's rationale for including highly liquid assets in the definition of money for Mexico. M_1 = M_2 + *bonos financieros, bonos hipotecarios, cédulas hipotecarias, titulos financieros,* savings deposits, other commercial paper, certificates of Nafinsa, general national and private savings bonds.

payments will adjust to the relative growth rates of money demand and domestically created stocks of money. If money demand grows faster than the Mexican authorities wish to expand the money supply via their own resources, then reserves flow inward. Another result is that reserves flow inward, not outward, in response to increase in real income and the general price level. Growth in domestic credit is related to reserve outflows, as is growth in the money multiplier. The interest rate effect is weak but conforms generally to the hypothesized signs.

Mexico experienced rapid growth during most of this period. Therefore reserves generally flowed inward, despite a worsening balance of trade. The policies of deficit financing adopted by the government kept the growth of domestic credit from becoming an overwhelming force on the balance of payments. The financial policies of the Central Bank, consistent with the general development policies, led to a stable reserve position for most of the period.

Experience and the implications of the model are clear for policy decisions tied to controlling the balance of payments. A restrictive monetary policy that maintains slow growth in domestic credit, allied with rapid growth in money demand, will generate reserve inflow, no matter what the movements in the balance of trade. This was the case during the early 1970s. The financial authorities attempted to slow money growth by using domestic controls in 1970, 1971, and 1972, with a resulting increase in foreign reserves. These reserves were required to maintain equilibrium in the money markets even though the authorities were attempting to depress reserves.

During the early period, implementation of Mexican monetary policy was simple because the world was not experiencing rapid inflation. After the world entered a period of inflation during the late 1960s and early 1970s, monetary policy could not be as easily administered. Guidelines had to adjust to the new period. An attempt to conform to the old guidelines led to foreign reserve inflows in 1970, 1971, 1972, and 1973. Restrictive monetary policy did little to decrease this stock of money in 1970, 1971, and 1972; since its implementation could only lead to a response in the balance of payments. If the policy of the Central Bank was to maintain equilibrium in the growth of payments stability, then it failed. If the aim of the financial authorities was to slow the growth in the money supply, it failed, just as would be predicted by the monetary approach to the balance of payments.

EXPANSION OF THE BASIC MODEL

Alternative specifications of the estimating equations can be developed. The money multiplier may be further defined as

$$a = \frac{1 + K}{(r^d + e) + K}$$

Equation (28) shows that this information can be incorporated into the model. We also earlier incorporated the insights of G. H. Borts and J. A. Hanson into the definition of domestic credit. From this alternative definition

$$\Delta D \equiv (Y_g - t - i_b)$$

where

      Y_g = government expenditures
      t = government fiscal revenues
      i_b = government borrowing

Finally, in equation (30) we incorporated this information into the monetary approach to the balance-of-payments model. One expects Y_g to have a negative effect on gR(R/H), and taxes and government borrowing should be positively related to growth in foreign reserves multiplied by reserves divided by high-powered money. In incorporating this relationship for D into the model, one must note that the original mathematical form of D as related to Y_g, t, and i_b is arithmetic. Since these are arithmetically related to the dependent variable of the model, no a priori information is available concerning the coefficients.

    Referring to equation (23), the money multiplier may be written

$$a = \frac{1 + K}{r + K}$$

where $r = r^d + e$. Taking the natural logarithm and differentiating with respect to time, we obtain the relationship

$$ga = gK\left(\frac{K(r - 1)}{K^2 + Kr + K + r}\right) - gr\left(\frac{r}{r + K}\right)$$

Incorporating this information into the model, the following estimation form is obtained:

$$(R/H)gR = a_1 gy - a_2 gi + \beta_1 gP - \beta_2 (D/H)gD$$
$$- \beta_3 gK\left(\frac{K(r - 1)}{K^2 + Kr + K + r}\right) + \beta_4 gr\left(\frac{r}{r + K}\right) + u \qquad (47)$$

Again one anticipates a_1 and β_1 to be positive and close to 1. The coefficients a_2 and β_2 are both expected to be negative and near -1. The coefficient β_3 is expected to be negative, while β_4 is anticipated to be positive. One knows nothing a priori about the sizes of β_3 and β_4. Estimation of the parameters was made for 1954–74. The results are

$$(R/H)gR = 0.662gy - 0.324gi + 0.994gP - 0.766(D/H)gD$$
$$\qquad (2.785) \quad (1.465) \qquad (4.578) \quad (-6.473)$$

$$+ \underset{(1.083)}{1.146gK} \left(\frac{K(r-1)}{K^2 + Kr + K + r} \right) + \underset{(4.85)}{1.046gr} \left(\frac{r}{r + K} \right) \qquad (47a)$$

$R^2 = .88$
$DW = 1.91$

The results of coefficients a_1, a_2, β_1, and β_2 are in agreement with earlier results. Only a_2, as usual, is significantly different from its hypothesized value. The coefficient β_3, however, is not significantly different from 0 and has the wrong sign, while β_4 is as anticipated from equation (47), with the sign and size correct and a high t-value. Overall, the regression has a significant F-level with $R^2 = .88$.

Referring to equation (31), the relationship for the change in domestic credit as related to government expenditures, taxes, and government borrowing is incorporated into the reserve flow equation. The estimating form of the equation is

$$(R/H)gR = a_1 gy - a_2 gi + \beta_1 gP - \beta_2 ga - \beta_3 (Y_g/H) + \beta_4 (t/H) + \beta_5 (i_b/H) + e \qquad (48)$$

The regression results are

$$(R/H)gR = 0.893gy - 0.006gi + 0.645gP - 0.803ga - 1.045(Y_g/H)$$
$$\qquad (2.934) \quad (0.030) \quad (3.156) \quad (-6.059) \quad (-10.041)$$

$$+ \underset{(9.406)}{1.054(t/H)} + \underset{(9.414)}{1.063(i_b/H)}$$

$R^2 = .92$
$DW = 2.03$

The sizes and signs of a_1, a_2, β_1, and β_2 are again as anticipated for the normal reserve flow equation. The coefficients β_3, β_4, and β_5 carry a negative, a positive, and a positive sign, respectively.

The empirical results of this regression are interesting. The signs of all the values except the interest rate are as predicted, giving strong evidence for the validity of the reserve flow equation for Mexico. The sizes of the coefficients are as expected, with a very high R^2. The expansion of the reduced form to include these different relationships allows us to obtain empirical tests on relevant policy equations. It is not our intention to use this empirical evidence to prove that D is at the mercy of the fiscal authorities; but the estimates on this equation for Y_g, t, and i_b constitute the empirical foundation for later analysis of the relationship of monetary policy to fiscal policy.

The definition of domestic credit in the form

$$D = \int_{t=0}^{t} Y_g dt - \int_{t=0}^{t} t dt - \int_{t=0}^{t} i_b dt$$

is useful, in that one may more easily delineate the causes of domestic credit creation. The differential form with respect to time (as in the reserve flow equation) is straightforward as to the effect of increased government expenditure upon reserve flows. The regression results show that an increase in government expenditure divided by high-powered money will result in an outflow of foreign reserves. Further, an increase in government revenue tends to cause reserve inflows. Again, an increase in government borrowing will stimulate reserve inflows similar in size to expenditure-stimulated outflows. The relationship of Y_g, t, and i_b is based upon their effect on the money supply. Where $Y_g > (t + i_b)$, there will necessarily be an increase in domestic credit. An increase in domestic credit, ceteris paribus, causes money supply to exceed money demand because H is increased. This causes the demand for goods, services, and assets to rise. Some of this increased demand will be met by the imports of goods, services, and assets. To purchase imported goods, the public buys foreign reserves from the Central Bank, thereby lowering R. Independently, if i_b or t increases, ceteris paribus, domestic credit falls and the opposite effect results with respect to reserves.

The mechanism by which these factors work on the reserve position is considered in subsequent chapters. If an increase in expenditures is met by government borrowing and/or fiscal revenue generation, then the net effect of domestic credit creation is zero. The act of increasing government expenditures will not necessarily result in a reserve outflow. The fact that in Mexico reserve outflows tend to be negatively related to government expenditures is explained by the federal fiscal and monetary structure. There are basically three ways for Mexican government expenditures to be financed: taxation, borrowing from the private sector (largely through the banking community), or Central Bank creation of domestic credit. The increase in government expenditure during the late 1950s and early 1960s was facilitated within strict guidelines that shifted the burden of government expenditure financing from increases in t to increases in i_b. When the government expenditure exceeded $t + i_b$, the remaining amount had to be financed by the Central Bank of Mexico. This form of financing would clearly cause domestically created assets to rise, thereby increasing the domestically created money stock. The increased domestically created money stock, ceteris paribus, would lead to a reserve outflow as money demand and money supply tended toward equilibrium.

We have argued that the policy implications of this model are such that reserves will grow if domestic credit is created at a rate below the rate of increase in money demand (assuming all other money supply factors are constant). Further, Mexico implemented this policy when it so desired by utilizing three variables: Y_g, t, and i_b. The variable Y_g is difficult for Mexico to regulate. With the present development policies, government expenditures have expanded at a rate greater than real growth. The policy of the 1950s and 1960s was import substitution, and the level of government expenditure was determined largely by the guideline of restraining expenditure growth to a rate only slightly greater than the growth in real income. The effect was to maintain a low rate of growth in domestic money creation (although it was positive in every year after 1956). Indeed, in 1956 domestic credit amounted to less than 25 percent of high-powered money, while by 1973 it accounted for 77 percent.

The ability of the government to finance its expenditures through fiscal revenue sources is developed in detail in Chapters 5 and 6. The historical relationship of the financial sector to economic development policy and fiscal revenue generation is developed in Chapter 4. The data indicate that the growing inability of the federal government to fund expenditures through taxation led to greater dependence upon the financial community to supply increasingly high levels of borrowed funds. These entered the reserve flow equation through i_b. As the government relied more upon borrowing to maintain a low level of increase in domestic credit, it evolved a financial structure that was less flexible as a tool for controlling i_b. As the ability of the Central Bank to control the levels of i_b (given expenditures and fiscal resources of the government) was impeded, its ability to control domestically created money was also lessened. Grasping the issue of the flexibility and performance of the government policies as they relate to t and i_b is crucial to the planner who utilizes the implications of the reserve flow equation to control reserves.

In a final empirical test of the reserve flow model, we include the expanded relationship of the money multiplier and the expanded relationship of the change in domestic credit. The estimating form is

$$(R/H)gR = a_1 gy - a_2 gi + \beta_1 gP - \beta_2 gK \left(\frac{K(r-1)}{K^2 + Kr + r + K} \right) + \beta_3 gr \left(\frac{r}{r+K} \right)$$

$$- \beta_4 (Y_g/H) + \beta_5 (t/H) + \beta_6 (i_b/H) + u \tag{49}$$

The results of the regression are

$$(R/H)gR = 0.777gy - 0.322gi + 1.015gP + 1.420gK\left(\frac{K(r-1)}{K^2 + Kr + r + K}\right)$$
$$\quad\quad (2.062) \quad (-1.356) \quad (3.819) \quad (1.010)$$

$$+ 1.007gr\left(\frac{r}{r+K}\right) - 0.739\left(\frac{Y_g}{H}\right) + 0.731\left(\frac{t}{H}\right) + 0.731\left(\frac{i_b}{H}\right) \quad (49a)$$
$$\quad\; (3.712) \quad\quad\;\; (-5.130) \quad\;\; (4.795) \quad\;\; (4.212)$$

$$R^2 = .885$$
$$DW = 1.96$$

These results of the fully expanded model are satisfactory. The sizes of a_1, a_2, and β_1 are not significantly different from 1, -1, and 1, respectively. The estimated results for coefficients β_2 and β_3 are mixed. The coefficient β_2 is positive and relatively large, but β_3 has the correct size and sign. Coefficients β_4, β_5, and β_6 are as expected and are consistent with the theoretical specification as well as with earlier empirical investigation. They are, however, somewhat smaller in size than expected.

One possible explanation for the low t-statistics on β_2 and β_3 may be due to a degree of multicollinearity. If this is the case, the standard errors of these coefficients would be biased upward, implying a downward bias in our t-values.

In retrospect the usefulness of the expanded equation is not in testing the validity of the reserve flow equation for Mexico (a fortiori, the stability of the money demand functions). It does, however, shed light on the factors that influence the domestically created money supply of Mexico. The ability of the reserve flow equation to explain the relationship of growth in foreign reserves to growth in domestic money demand and domestic money supply is clear for annual data from equation (49a). The expansion of the model to include the broadened definition of the money multiplier and domestic credit further elucidates the effects of particular policy variables.

QUARTERLY RESULTS

The regressions are also estimated by using quarterly data for 1960–74. The year 1960 is selected because of limited availability of data for series prior to that year. Specifically, there exists no officially published series of quarterly income data. Indeed, the series used in the following analysis was obtained from an unpublished work of the Economics Section of the Bank of Mexico. The data used to test the model for quarterly data are

y_p = permanent income, a geometric weighted average of present and past income
P = consumer price index
D = domestic credit
i = interest rate (long-term) in Mexico
i_{us} = interest rate (long-term) in United States
a = money multiplier
r = reserve-to-deposit ratio
R = international reserve held by the Bank of Mexico
M_1 = nominal money supply
M_1/P = real money supply

First, equations are estimated for both real and nominal money demand. The estimating forms of real and nominal money demand, respectively, are

$$g(M_1/P) = a_1 gy_p - a_2 gi + u \tag{50}$$

$$g(M_1) = a_1 gy_p - a_2 gi + \beta_1 gP + u' \tag{51}$$

where u' is a stochastic disturbance term.

The regression results are reported in Table 3.8 for 1961–74. Regressions 1 and 2 are for real money demand, and regressions 3 and 4 are for nominal money demand. Regressions 1 and 3 use the Mexican long-term rate of interest and regressions 2 and 4 use the U.S. rate of return on one-year issues of selected notes and bonds.

Several conclusions may be drawn from Table 3.8. The F-levels are not all significant. The permanent income elasticities of money demand are all close to the hypothesized values, have the correct sign, and are significant. The rate of growth in the interest rate appears to be insignificant in determining money demand, although the signs are correct. The results are similar to those for the annual results in Table 3.6, with price elasticities not significantly different from the anticipated values. From this evidence we cannot reject the hypothesis that money demand is linearly homogeneous in prices. The hypothesis that $\beta_1 = 1$ is accepted. Close examination of regression 4, which is the most germane to this study, shows that the quarterly regressions perform satisfactorily. The F-value is significant at the .01 level and the DW indicates no significant autocorrelation. The only disappointing factor is the $R^2 = .19$.

The estimating equation for the reserve flow equation is

$$(R/H)gR = a_1 gy_p - a_2 gi + \beta_1 gP - \beta_2 ga - \beta_3 (D/H)gD + u' \tag{52}$$

where u' is a stochastic disturbance term.

TABLE 3.8

Estimated Mexican Money Demand Equations, Quarterly, 1961–74

$$g(M_1/P) = a_1 gy_p - a_2 gi + u$$
$$g(M_1) = a_1 gy_p - a_2 gi + \beta_1 gP + u'$$

	Equation			
	1	2	3	4
Variable	$g(M_1/P)$	$g(M_1/P)$	$g(M_1)$	$g(M_1)$
Permanent income elasticity of money demand	0.977	1.003	0.942	1.013
	(3.946)	(3.989)	(3.236)	(3.425)
Mexican interest rate elasticity of money demand	−0.071		−0.089	
	(−0.558)		(−0.664)	
U.S. interest rate elasticity of money demand		−0.069		−0.071
		(−0.909)		(−0.896)
β_1			1.101	1.037
			(4.231)	(4.174)
R^2	.01	.03	.19	.19
F	.52	1.16	5.92	6.18
DW	1.93	1.93	1.77	1.86

Note: The t-statistic is reported in parentheses.
Source: Compiled by the author.

Again, we anticipate both a_1 and β_1 to take the value of $+1$; β_3 should take the value of -1; and the sign of a_2 is predicted to be negative.

Estimation of equation (52) for the second quarter of 1961 to the fourth quarter of 1974 yields

$$(R/H)gR = 0.633gy_p - 0.120gi + 0.552gP - 0.684ga - 0.552(D/H)gD$$
$$(2.865) \quad (-1.231) \quad (2.732) \quad (-6.314) \quad (-5.222)$$

$R^2 = .461$
$F = 10.67$
$DW = 2.01$

The equation results are satisfactory. The F-level is significant at $a = .01$ and the R^2 shows about half of the variation explained. The signs of the various coefficients are all correct, and the t-statistics indicate that all coefficients are significant except that of the growth in the interest rate. The only disappointing factor is the size of the coefficients β_1, β_2, and β_3, which are all less than the hypothesized values. Both a_1 and β_1 are not significantly different from 1. The coefficients for β_2 and β_3, however, are not in the interval around 1 at the $a = .05$ level.

The inclusion of the U.S. interest as a proxy for the world does not significantly change the results. Again the growth in the rate of interest is insignificant with relation to gR(R/H). The results are

$$(R/H)gR = 0.662gy_p - 0.808gi + 0.502gP - 0.685ga - 0.558(D/H)gD$$
$$(2.895) \quad (-0.141) \quad (2.495) \quad (-6.233) \quad (-5.420)$$

$$R^2 = .445$$
$$F = 10.00$$
$$DW = 1.979$$

and are not significantly different from the results in equation (52). Again, all of the signs are correct, t-statistics high except for a_2, and the values of the coefficients relatively low.

NOTES

1. Clark Reynolds, *The Mexican Economy* (New Haven: Yale University Press, 1970), pp. 286–88.

2. Robert L. Bennett, *The Financial Sector and Economic Development* (Baltimore: Johns Hopkins, 1965), p. 133.

3. Raymond W. Goldsmith, *The Financial Development of Mexico* (Paris: OECD, 1966), p. 55.

4. Antonio Gómez Oliver, "La política monetaria y el nivel de precios en México," working paper, Centro de Estudios Monetarios Latinamericanos, 1974, pp. 35–40. Gómez used annual observations for 1934–40 and 1948–73. An interesting point of his study, which is verified by our results, is that the expected rate of inflation is statistically insignificant (p. 44) with respect to money demand. In his study the signs were correct (negative) but t-values less than 0.1. Tests by the present author yielded similar results, although several methods of calculation of expected rates of inflation were used.

CHAPTER

4

FISCAL REVENUE POLICY
IN MEXICO

An analysis of the fiscal revenue structure is presented, since one may contend that fiscal policy since the late 1950s has played a prominent role in determining how monetary policies are conducted, as well as the end to which these policies are aimed. More specifically, it is argued that a relatively income-inelastic revenue structure has played a prominent role in determining the financial structure and policies of the 1970s. Indeed, it will be maintained that the inability of the authorities to mobilize internal resources in conjunction with fiscal forces led to the rapid expansion in domestic credit by the Central Bank during the 1970s.

Nicholas Kaldor states:

> The importance of public revenue to the underdeveloped countries can hardly be exaggerated if they are to achieve their hopes of accelerated economic progress. Whatever the prevailing ideology or political colour of a particular government, it must steadily expand a whole host of nonrevenue-yielding services—education, health, communication systems, and so on—as a prerequisite to a country's economic and cultural development.[1]

Mexico's development policy since the 1950s has emphasized import-substitution policies that have had a negative impact upon the generation of public resources

---

Much of the analysis in this chapter appears in D. S. Wilford and W. T. Wilford, "Fiscal Revenues in Mexico: A Measure of Performances, 1950-73," *Public Finance* 31, no. 1 (1976): 103–15.

through tax policy. As a result, the nation has relied increasingly upon the nontax financial sector—private savings and monetizing the deficit—for financing federal expenditures. Gilberto Escobedo comments:

> As the public financial requirements were increased, mainly because of incapacity to increase tax revenues at the same rate as public expenditures . . . the Bank of Mexico had to tolerate greater increases in the money supply.[2]

The financing of new government debt is becoming increasingly difficult for Mexico. This is due in part to the result of the import-substitution policies and accompanying reliance upon fiscal incentives and income tax concessions, and deemphasis of imports and the tax base associated therewith. Further, the inability of revenues to keep pace with expenditures places the responsibility of debt financing upon the nontax financial sector. Since the 1950s the Mexican government has increased its dependency upon the nontax financial sector for funding federal expenditures, a situation that results, at least in part, from the inability of the public sector to generate sufficient yields from tax resources. Escobedo claims that the federal government should no longer depend upon transfers of savings from the financial sector to the government for payment of expenditures. He hypothesizes that the cost of such transfers is becoming increasingly high for the Mexican banking system and that the marshaling of resources through tax policy is of paramount importance for stable economic growth.[3] One policy alternative to monetizing the federal debt is, of course, resource mobilization through the tax structure.

The purpose of this chapter is to measure Mexican fiscal revenue performance during 1950-73 and 1958-73 by evaluating fiscal responsiveness to economic growth. The years 1958-73 were selected as a period in which Mexican policy was directed at a concerted import-substitution industrial development, and efforts to improve the enforcement features of the tax structure through simplification of tax statutes and through institution building in tax collection offices. Comparison of the two periods permits an evaluation of self-help performance during 1958-73, a period in which the dual goals of import substitution and simplified tax legislation and enforcement created divergent influences on the revenue structure.

REVENUE PERFORMANCE CRITERION

To evaluate the historic fiscal response in Mexico, we shall examine the ability of its tax structure to generate proportionately higher revenues both through discretionary action (tax rate and base changes, legislative action, improvement in collection techniques) and through revenue growth that is automatically marshaled with rising economic activity. This measure is identified as the revenue performance criterion, and may be broadly defined as the ability of a revenue structure to generate, from whatever sources, increased government revenues for current and capital expenditures during the process of economic growth. The pressure for increased revenues to finance GNP-elastic demands for social goods and services requires that revenues increase at a rate higher than that of growth in income; that is, the overall revenue-income elasticity coefficient (ξ) for a revenue structure must be elastic. The broad measure is shown below.[4]

$$\xi = \frac{\text{percent change in revenue}}{\text{percent change in GNP}} > 1$$

In quantifying the revenue performance criterion of a region, one is not concerned about the source of the alteration in tax yields (whether from national income-related or exogenous influences) but, rather, about the overall ability of the source to stimulate proportionately higher revenues with regard to economic development, regardless of the factors encouraging that growth. The revenue performance criterion is, therefore, measured by the historic aggregate responsiveness of the structure as income increases. The criterion permits an evaluation of the national effort to stimulate resources under conditions of growth, but it does not measure the responsiveness of revenues to income changes alone.[5] This chapter analyzes the historic income responsiveness of disaggregated components of the Mexican revenue system in order to determine the revenue-income elasticity of the revenue base as a whole, as well as to ascertain the responsiveness of individual tax sources.

STRUCTURE OF THE REVENUE SYSTEM IN MEXICO

Table 4.1 gives the percentage contributions of the various sources to total receipts for 1950, 1958, and 1973. The data show that total tax receipts declined dramatically in their percentage contribution to revenue. In 1950 almost 80 percent of the total Mexican revenue was tax-generated, while in 1973 it was only 59 percent, indicating a relative decline of 25 percent. While the relative contribution of "other ordinary revenues" (charges for public services, income from public property, and so forth) showed some upward trend between 1950 and 1958, overall decline of these revenues occurred during the period, from 20 percent in 1950 to 7 percent in 1973 (Table 4.1). Clearly the major increase in funding for Mexican federal expenditures was borrowing, which increased from zero in 1950 to 33 percent in 1973. The aggregate data are, therefore, disheartening to the policy maker who views as important the necessity to relieve pressure on the financial community through increased tax revenues.

TABLE 4.1

Mexico: Percent Distribution of Current Revenue Sources, 1950, 1958, and 1973

Revenue Source	1950	1958	1973
Total receipts	100.00	100.00	100.00
Total tax receipts*	79.91	65.02	59.80
Income	20.53	21.19	25.35
Exploitation of natural resources	4.76	2.83	.84
Manufacture, sale, possession, and use of industrial products	14.14	11.43	11.68
Sales tax	9.71	6.81	12.40
Imports	12.53	12.19	6.08
Exports	14.64	8.59	1.22
Insurance premiums	.25	.261	.24
Lotteries and games	.66	.56	.27
Other ordinary revenue	20.09	26.30	7.42
Total tax receipts plus other ordinary revenue	100.00	91.32	67.22
Borrowing	0.00	8.68	32.72

*Only selected categories of tax revenue are listed.

Source: Statistics of the Mexican Economy (Mexico City: Nacional Financiera, 1974).

On a more positive note, the traditionally income-elastic personal and corporate income tax receipts increased from 21 percent of Mexican revenues in 1950 to 25 percent in 1973. Indeed, as a percentage of total tax receipts, the income tax yields rose from 26 percent in 1950 to 42 percent in 1973; this indicates some success in restructuring the tax base so that there is less reliance upon indirect sources such as imports and exports. The increased importance of income taxes in the structure, however, is far less than one would expect for a country whose dependence upon import-export levies decreased dramatically with the implementation of import-substitution policies during the late 1950s.

Table 4.1 shows that the second area of significant tax improvement was receipts from the sales taxes, which contributed 12 percent of total taxes in 1950 and rose to 21 percent in 1973. The relative increase in sales taxes reflects Mexican development strategy, since sales taxes are easier to collect in emerging nations than taxes on manufacturing and on income. The increased reliance upon sales taxes may be attributed to the inability of the fiscal authorities to marshal taxes through more income-elastic structures, such as personal and corporate income levies. Contrary to some observations, however, sales taxes in Mexico do not appear as inelastic as one might hypothesize. C. H. McClure, Jr., has argued:

> The indirect tax system of almost any developing country will of necessity include a broad-based tax on consumption. Such taxes are likely to be regressive, as consumption falls as a fraction of income as income rises. . . . Perhaps the best way to do this [introduce more progressivity] is to exempt from the broad-based tax those items of consumption that figure especially heavily in the market basket of very low income families. Most obvious among the candidates for exemption on this ground are cereal grains and simple food products fabricated from them. . . .[6]

Our observation of the Mexican data, as will be delineated, suggests that built-in exemptions for basic foodstuffs, clothing, and shelter tend to generate a much higher revenue-income elasticity for sales taxes than one would a priori expect. In short, it is not possible to enforce collection from small shops, street vendors, and itinerant marketplace sellers that account for a substantial portion of both money and barter exchange. Since the bulk of low-income purchases are made from these groups, the sales tax elasticity is accordingly higher. This observation is reflected not only in the Mexican data but also in studies that estimate the sales tax revenue-income elasticity for other Latin American nations.*

In addition to reliance upon indirect tax sources, Mexico suffers from many of the other fiscal structure problems typical of Latin American nations. Clark Reynolds comments:

> Tax collection is much more difficult in Latin America than, for example, in northern Europe or the United States where qualified administrative personnel are more readily available, higher salaries provide less incentive for graft, and society is conditioned to accept a higher incidence of taxation without protest. Still, there is reason to criticize the failure of Mexican tax policy to keep pace with the

---

*The Mexican revenue-income elasticity performance measure does not permit precise evaluation of the regressivity of the sales tax because the revenue data utilized capture the effect of rate and base changes over time. However, in another study of the sales tax performance for the five countries constituting the Central American Common Market during 1955–74, the author utilized a methodology to adjust the sales tax data for exogenous rate and base changes. Even the adjusted revenue-income elasticities for these five countries were surprisingly high: 1.09 for Guatemala, 1.42 for Honduras, 1.47 for Nicaragua, 1.41 for Costa Rica, and 1.09 for El Salvador. See D. S. Wilford and W. T. Wilford, "Measuring Fiscal Self-Help in Central America: An Assessment of the Responsiveness of the Revenue Structure to Economic Growth in the Common Market," in J. Toye, ed., *Taxation and Development* (London: Frank Cass, 1978).

growing demands for public expenditures that one would expect to accompany the rapid pace of development, urbanization, and social change that Mexico has experienced since 1940. Mexico's fiscal performance has been far from adequate to support even the most modest revenue requirements as revealed by national comparison.[7]

Reynolds also contends that "import substitution policies, as they reduce the traded share of output, tend to lower the government's capacity to tax,"[8] an observation certainly applicable to the Mexican experience. Tax laws are used as an inducement for increased investment through both favorable income tax treatment and reduced tariffs for capital and intermediate material imports. The import-substitution development path itself has imposed restrictions on the Mexican ability to raise revenues, and income tax collections have suffered from fiscal incentives income tax concessions.

Timothy King points out the relation of import-substituting industries to the tax structure and suggests using the relationship as a method of subsidizing these industries. He notes that tax exemptions and government subsidies are not perfect substitutes, but proceeds to elucidate how exemptions are pervasive in the Mexican economy. With respect to the powers of the authorities, he says:

In Mexico tax-exemption policies have been directed primarily at import-substituting industries. There are two separate schemes. A long series of legislation, going back to 1926, has been operated mainly by the Ministries of Finance and Industry and Trade, and is intended to promote manufacturing industries. Apart from this legislation, the Ministry of Finance is empowered to reduce taxes for any industry for a wide variety of objectives. In terms of the total relief from taxation given, this latter scheme is more important than the detailed and elaborate tax-exemption legislation.[9]

In short, although the government is attempting through its legislative program to move to a more progressive income tax base, the import-substitution development plan requires a comparatively regressive indirect tax structure.

MEASURING THE RESPONSIVENESS OF TAX REVENUE TO ECONOMIC GROWTH

The revenue performance criterion measures the responsiveness of the fiscal structure to increases in GNP. Let

R_i = revenue from the ith source
δ = a constant

Y = gross national product

ξ = the revenue-income elasticity coefficient

μ = a log normally distributed error term

Calculation of ξ over time for each revenue source provides an estimate of the revenue performance criterion. Taking logs,

$$\ln R_j = \delta_j + \xi_j \ln Y + \mu_j$$

The values of δ and ξ are given in Table 4.2 for 1950-73 and in Table 4.3 for 1958-73. The tables show revenue performance for the following categories: income; manufacture, sale, possession, and use of industrial products; natural resources exploitation; sales; import; export; lotteries and games; other ordinary revenue; total tax revenue. The R^2s are all high except for exports, a result that we expect a priori, since for Mexico exports are more a function of world market conditions than of domestic income. The t-statistics are reported in parentheses below their respective coefficients, and autocorrelation adjustment is performed where required in both tables. All revenue-income elasticity values are significant ($a = .05$), except for exports in Table 4.3.

The elasticities for 1950-73 are generally as expected, with income tax yields showing the highest (1.311). The elasticity for the income tax is heartening, since Mexico seeks to redirect its structure from reliance upon export and import revenues (27 percent of total revenues in 1950) to dependence upon the internal sector. Sales taxes were also high, with an elasticity of 1.127. Exports showed the lowest (.207), and the coefficient for natural resource levies was also low (.583). Since exploitation of natural resources (primarily oil) will become increasingly important in the development plans of Mexico, and thus in its fiscal structure, one would expect the revenue-income responsiveness to be increased from this source. Some federal receipts from natural resources taxation are not captured in this category but are entered as "other ordinary income," a category whose ξ is not much higher (.705). Import taxes, which contributed 6.08 percent of total revenue in 1973, recorded a historic ξ approximating unity during 1950-73.

The export revenue category for 1958-73 shows a ξ that is both small and insignificant, anticipated a priori since Mexican legislative direction during the period was aimed at lowering export taxes in order to promote industrial expansion. The import ξ fell slightly, to .992 during 1958-73, while the major gainers in ξ were sales taxes (1.286 in 1950-73 and 1.403 for 1958-73) and income taxes (1.311 and 1.446). The natural resource ξ increased slightly, although it remained rather unresponsive.

Examination of the two tables permits some generalizations on the Mexican fiscal revenue structure during the post-1950 period of dramatic economic growth. The most income-responsive sources are, as expected, income and sales taxes. Although one would anticipate a high ξ for income levies, the 1.311 coefficient did not produce a major shift in the tax burden toward direct taxes. In 1950 income taxes amounted to only 1.82 percent of total GNP, and by 1973 they represented only 4 percent. By comparison, the United States figure is approximately 16 percent for federal income taxes alone. Although income-elastic in the Mexican revenue structure, the low weight of income levies in the tax structure suggests that they cannot contribute significantly to the ξ of the system.

Much of the improved revenue yield from income taxes has been the result of better enforcement. Nonarbitrary enforcement, however, is not a historic pattern in Latin America; and Mexico is no exception. Not only are there social and cultural influences mitigating the enforcement of income tax laws, but another barrier is built into the development plan in the form of corporate tax incentive concessions to encourage industrial location. Foreign investors have been offered tax advantages for specific categories of investment, and domestic investors are frequently offered tax-free status for sectoral investments. All of these incentives reduce corporate income tax yields, but they are viewed as necessary for the import-substitution programs. Reynolds notes that attempts to foster investment through tax incentives have led to an almost casual attitude toward auditing corporate accounts. As a result, a great deal of the tax burden has fallen on the urban middle class. For this group the tax structure appears to be progressive and the administration strict. However, above the middle-income category, the taxes become regressive, since personal income is now often treated as business income.

While the historic sales tax yields in Mexico appear to be income-responsive, they are generally regarded as relatively income-inelastic in developed fiscal structures. The ability of Mexico to maintain a high ξ from this source (1.4 for 1958–73) in the future undoubtedly will be lessened, and the ξ should fall as growth continues. Past performance of sales tax ξ is due at least in part to structural changes that have upper limits, including broad exceptions for basic consumer goods that pass through merchants who do not collect taxes. That loophole, which contributes to higher ξ, will close as more sophisticated trading develops, and the sales tax elasticity will probably assume the characteristic of the developed nations.

Though increasing in percentage contribution to revenue since 1950, direct taxes have managed to do little more than offset the decline in the import contribution. The overall direct tax income elasticity was 1.132 for 1950–73 and 1.274 for 1958–73, illustrating close to unit elasticity in the revenue structure over both periods. Countries with low per capita tax burdens are expected to exhibit a higher direct tax elasticity than has been demonstrated in Mexico. This did not occur in Mexico at least partially because of import-substitution development policies.

TABLE 4.2

Revenue-Income Responsiveness: Mexico, 1950–73

Revenue Source	Regression No.	Constant	Income Elasticity	R^2	F-Value	DW	RHO
Income taxes	1	-5.214 (-17.741)	1.311 (36.185)	.99	2,771.35	2.03	0.330
Manufacture, sale, and use of industrial products	2	-4.941 (-11.982)	1.127 (14.249)	.98	1,764.16	1.99	0.756
Natural resources exploitation	3	-4.093 (-7.938)	0.583 (5.861)	.80	85.188	2.29	0.316
Sales tax	4	-6.095 (-9.502)	1.286 (10.488)	.98	1,068.84	1.23	0.823
Import tax	5	-4.606 (-18.736)	1.037 (21.886)	.98	1,171.53	1.85	0.400
Export tax	6	-1.045 (-2.329)	0.207 (2.387)	.57	26.56	1.80	0.758 -0.245
Lotteries and games	7	-7.097 (-31.380)	0.928 (21.297)	.98	1,578.06	1.83	0.409
Other ordinary revenue	8	-2.731 (-7.336)	0.705 (9.810)	.80	84.76	2.04	-0.167
Total tax receipts	9	-3.232 (-11.580)	1.132 (21.267)	.99	7,352.48	1.82	0.848

Note: The t-statistics are in parentheses.
Source: Compiled by the author.

TABLE 4.3

Revenue-Income Responsiveness: Mexico, 1958–73

Revenue Source	Regression No.	Constant	Income Elasticity	R^2	F-Value	DW	RHO
Income taxes	1	−5.987 (−32.215)	1.446 (43.470)	.99	2,471.85	2.08	−0.151
Manufacture, sale, and use of industrial products	2	−6.472 (−13.725)	1.394 (16.559)	.98	873.63	1.81	0.455
Natural resources exploitation	3	−5.220 (−6.524)	0.785 (5.496)	.92	164.70	2.18	0.538
Sales tax	4	−6.947 (−31.341)	1.403 (35.339)	.97	513.17	1.47	−0.747 −0.287
Import tax	5	−4.351 (−6.489)	0.992 (8.295)	.96	320.86	1.80	.529
Export tax	6	0.189 (0.475)	−0.019 (−0.265)	.06	0.761	1.88	0.028
Lotteries and games	7	−7.094 (−13.007)	0.927 (9.522)	.97	531.51	1.82	0.469
Other ordinary revenue	8	−3.591 (−6.203)	0.853 (8.233)	.83	63.42	1.57	−0.430
Total tax receipts	9	−4.091 (−21.755)	1.274 (38.065)	.99	17,665.83	1.80	0.685

Note: The t-statistics are in parentheses.
Source: Compiled by the author.

69

Ironically, as indicated in Table 4.1, casual observation suggests that the revenue with the highest elasticity has been federal borrowing. It would be desirable for Mexican planners to face an income-elastic tax structure to help alleviate the growing problem of increased federal borrowing. However, this study concludes that the overall nonborrowed revenue structure is only unit-elastic in its income responsiveness, and that the modest improvement in income elasticity has been barely sufficient to offset losses in import levies. Income taxation and enforcement powers are limited by built-in constraints of the development plan and enforcement barriers; and other revenue sources are not reliable for rapid revenue growth, since many of them are relatively income-inelastic.

In summary, the revenue structure in Mexico is much less income-responsive than one would desire for a country in the process of developing. As larger portions of the national economy become dependent upon government infrastructure expenditures, and as the need for social goods and services expands, Mexico faces a tax structure that will finance a decreasing percentage of federal outlays. The tendency will, therefore, be toward monetizing the debt. It is concluded that, under the existing Mexican tax system, it will be difficult for the government to increase the revenues required to maintain the demand for social goods associated with historic Mexican economic growth, unless the restriction placed upon the fiscal revenue-generating structure changes. Since the developmental policy of the 1950s and 1960s has been important in creating this structure, it is difficult to expect changes in the fiscal revenue collection structure without change in the policies of development.

NOTES

1. Nicholas Kaldor, "Will Underdeveloped Countries Learn to Tax?" in *Essays on Economic Policy*, Nicholas Kaldor, ed. (London: G. Duckworth, 1964), p. 225.

2. Gilberto Escobedo, "Ahorro y desarrollo económico," Bank of Mexico, mimeographed, 1973, p. 13.

3. Ibid., p. 18.

4. See H. M. Groves and C. H. Kahn, "The Stability of State and Local Tax Yields," *American Economic Review* 40 (March 1952): 87–102; W. T. Wilford, "State Tax Stability Criteria and the Revenue-Income Elasticity Coefficient Reconsidered," *National Tax Journal* 17 (September 1965): 304–12; W. V. Williams, R. M. Anderson, D. O. Froehle, and K. L. Lamb, "The Stability, Growth, and Stabilizing Influence of State Taxes," ibid. 26 (1974): 267–74; and W. T. Wilford, "Comment on Stability, Growth, and Stabilizing Influence of State Taxes," ibid. 27, no. 4 (December 1975): 452–59.

5. For a more detailed analysis of the revenue performance criterion see D. Sykes Wilford and Walton T. Wilford, "The Revenue-Income Elasticity Coefficient: Performance and Stability Criteria," *Review of Business and Economic Research* 12, no. 2 (Winter 1976–77): 90–93.

6. C. H. McClure, Jr., "The Proper Use of Indirect Taxation in Latin America," *Public Finance/Finances publiques* 30, no. 1 (1975): 23.

7. Clark Reynolds, *The Mexican Economy* (New Haven: Yale University Press, 1970), p. 275.

8. Ibid., p. 272.

9. Timothy King, *Mexico, Industrialization and Trade Policies Since 1940* (London: Oxford University Press, 1970), p. 99.

CHAPTER

5

THE MONEY SUPPLY IN
MEXICO: THE ROLE OF
THE MONETARY AUTHORITIES

A number of studies on Mexican monetary policy have been conducted. Nevertheless, controversy persists regarding the tools and effects of policy actions taken by the authorities.[1] In the ensuing analysis we shall abstract from the views of various authors, as well as our own work, in order to investigate the mechanisms available to the monetary authorities. The issues upon which we shall focus are twofold. First, what variables can the Central Bank control? Second, can authorities actually control the money stock within sufficiently narrow limits to implement a particular economic policy? In order to thoroughly examine these two issues, a detailed review of the money supply process for Mexico is required. This chapter focuses on both issues.

The purpose of this chapter is to study the Mexican money supply process. In an analysis of the procedures and capabilities of the authorities to influence the money stock, cogent information from the monetary approach to the balance of payments is employed. The analysis is divided into three main parts. The first section deals with the Central Bank's role in controlling domestic variables, including domestic credit and the money multiplier. The second section concerns the inability of the authorities to control prices and interest rates, while the third reviews the policies of the authorities since 1954.

DOMESTIC VARIABLES

The two major domestic operative policy variables for the Mexican authorities are domestic credit, defined as "other assets – other liabilities," and the money multiplier. Authorities can directly or indirectly influence the variables through monetary policy and/or fiscal policy options. The Central Bank can explicitly control domestic credit and can strongly influence the money multiplier.

The Central Bank of Mexico

Article 28 of the Mexican Political Constitution states that issuance of bank notes remains the right of a single agency of the Mexican government: the Banco de México. In 1917 the Constitutional Congress expressly provided for the establishment of the Banco de México, but not until 1925 did the Central Bank begin to emerge from the myriad existing private financial institutions. In the Banco de México Organic Law of 1936, the Central Bank finally obtained full control of monetary reserves and had authority over the issuance and placement of bank notes. In 1941 it became even more powerful with the enactment of the Legal Reserve Requirement Law, which conceded it legal command over reserves. Other banking laws of the 1940s and early 1950s, along with those of 1970, established the bank's role of adviser and executor of monetary policy, but reserved final responsibility for such policy to the federal government.

The growth of the Mexican Central Bank is similar to that of the U.S. Federal Reserve System, with some significant exceptions. Whereas the Federal Reserve Act of 1913 was designed to establish the Federal Reserve System as an agency semiindependent from the government, the Bank of Mexico was established as an integral part of the federal government. Thus, government and bank policies are considered synonymous, and consequently the Central Bank may be viewed as an essential arm of the federal government's overall policy objectives. However, in some instances the Central Bank resembles the Federal Reserve System in that both are responsible for initiating and advising the executive authority on monetary policy issues. The Bank of Mexico, like the Federal Reserve System, can set required reserve ratios for commercial banks and other financial intermediaries. The Central Bank issues paper currency that is a liability of the bank, just as Federal Reserve notes are liabilities of the U.S. Federal Reserve System. The diurnal functions of the two banks are similar, in that both are clearinghouses for daily activities of the banking community and both may act as the banker of the federal government. Though the Federal Reserve System and the Central Bank of Mexico both carry government and community bank deposits, only the Central Bank deals directly with the public by making loans or holding personal demand deposits.

One of the most important administrative functions of the Bank of Mexico is selective allocation of credit via its various policy tools. While both systems act as the clearinghouse for government bonds, only the Mexican Central Bank uses required reserves as an effective tool to promote bond purchases. The discount window of the Federal Reserve is used to provide liquidity for banks, and in some instances to attempt to influence the interest rates, whereas the Central Bank of Mexico actively uses the discount window selectively to increase liquidity among banks, sectors, and regions. In short, the Central Bank acts as a director and executor of government financial and monetary policy in a developing country, while the Federal Reserve System is the autonomous initiator, director, and executor of monetary policy in an economy that is developed and that plays a unique role in the world monetary system. Therefore, one would expect their positions and roles to differ in those areas dealing with the promotion of economic development. To interpret the Central Bank of Mexico's control over its monetary environment, a detailed survey of domestic credit creation as it relates to the bank follows.

Domestic Credit Creation and the Central Bank

The monetary authorities create domestic credit when the Treasury withdraws deposits from the Central Bank, the government transfers Treasury deposits from the Central Bank to the private banking sector, the Central Bank creates commercial bank deposits, or the private sector moves deposits from the Central Bank to the private banking system. Therefore, while it cannot by itself create money, the Central Bank can provide the vehicle and select the path for money creation. Either the government or the private sector, in conjunction with the Central Bank, must act to alter the level of domestic credit. As with the Federal Reserve System, the Central Bank can decrease domestic credit through selling securities to the government, selling securities to the private sector, calling in loans from businesses, individuals, or banks. The Central Bank of Mexico differs from the Federal Reserve System in that the latter no longer directly calls in loans from the private sector.

The Central Bank, therefore, can directly alter its portfolio of domestically created assets, including private and public loans, and private and public securities. In 1962, for example, most domestic credit was associated with business and individual loans made by the Bank of Mexico, while in 1973 domestic credit was generated primarily through purchases of government securities. The Treasury can also affect domestic credit by reallocating its deposits between the commercial banks and the Central Bank, a situation that also exists in the Federal Reserve System. Finally, the Mexican private sector can influence the domestic credit position by reallocating its demand deposit accounts between private banks and the Central Bank.

Examination of a typical but hypothetical set of balance sheets will illuminate the process by which the Central Bank may alter domestic credit. Table 5.1 presents balance sheets for the Central Bank, the federal government, and the private sector. From the table it is evident that there exists 100 million pesos in domestically created credit. High-powered money (defined as coins and currency in circulation, plus bank reserves) is distributed between 100 million pesos in notes and coins and 400 million pesos in reserves held by the banking community. Foreign reserves are 400 million pesos. Therefore, assets other than foreign reserves (OA), minus liabilities other than high-powered money (OL), equals 100 million pesos. Assume that the Central Bank decides to purchase a

TABLE 5.1

Period 1: Consolidated Balance Sheets of the Mexican Central Bank, the Federal Government, and Private Banking System
(million pesos)

Assets		Liabilities	
Central Bank			
Foreign reserves	400	High-powered money	500
Government bonds	200	Treasury deposits	300
Bank securities	200	Business and individual deposits	200
Direct loans			
Government	100		
Bank	50		
Business and individual	50		
Total direct loans	200		
Total assets	1,000	Total liabilities	1,000
Federal Government			
Treasury deposits at		Government bonds	200
Central Bank	300	Government loans	100
Total assets	300	Total liabilities	300
Private Banking System			
Reserve deposits at		Private demand deposits	400
Central Bank	400		
Total assets	400	Total liabilities	400

Source: Compiled by the author.

new issue of government bonds worth 200 million pesos. Treasury deposits increase by 200 million pesos and the government's balance sheet is readjusted. Note that there is no increase in domestic credit or high-powered money because OA - OL remains unchanged through offsetting increases in assets and liabilities. Therefore, the Central Bank's purchase of government bonds does not necessarily imply domestic credit creation. If the Treasury lowers its deposits at the Central Bank by 200 million pesos, the OL falls, government deposits at local banks increase, and bank reserves deposited at the Central Bank or currency must increase. Thus, OA - OL increases by 200 million pesos.

Now allow the Central Bank to extend credit of 100 million pesos to banks through its direct loan mechanism used to promote regional bank growth. Assets of the Central Bank increase by 100 million pesos; liabilities of the Central

TABLE 5.2

Period 2: Consolidated Balance Sheets of the Mexican Central Bank, the Federal Government, and Private Banking System
(million pesos)

Assets		Liabilities	
Central Bank			
Foreign reserves	400	High-powered money	900
Government bonds	400	Treasury deposits	300
Bank securities	200	Business and individual	200
Direct loans			
Government	100		
Bank	150		
Business and individual	150		
Total direct loans	400		
Total assets	1,400	Total liabilities	1,400
Federal Government			
Treasury deposits at		Government bonds	400
Central Bank	300	Government loans	100
Deposits in private banks	200		
Total assets	500	Total liabilities	500
Private Banking System			
Reserve deposits at		Demand deposits	
Central Bank	800	Private	600
		Government	200
		Total demand deposits	800
Total assets	800	Total liabilities	800

Source: Compiled by the author.

Bank, in the form of high-powered money, increase by 100 million pesos. Thus, assets of the private banking system increase by 100 million pesos, thereby allowing the system to create new demand deposits of an equal amount (assuming a money multiplier of 1). The money supply has increased by 100 million pesos, as has domestic credit.

Alternatively, the Central Bank may expand credit by loaning to business and individuals either by direct project loans or by discounting. Let the Central Bank increase its business and individual loans by 100 million pesos. Further assume that the new loans are deposited (either spent in the private sector or deposited directly) in commercial banks rather than in the Central Bank. Table 5.2

represents the new set of circumstances after the previous three actions of the bank.

Table 5.2 presents a set of circumstances in which there are 400 million pesos in foreign reserves and 500 million pesos in domestic credit. The domestic credit was created through all three avenues open to the Central Bank: the federal government, the private banking community, and the private business or individual. Domestic credit increased by a total of 400 million pesos, as did high-powered money (recall $H = R + D$); and, given a money multiplier of 1, the money supply subsequently increased by 400 million pesos.

Assume that the money supply and money demand were in equilibrium when the increase in domestic credit was initiated by the authorities. Ceteris paribus, the increase in domestic credit would now cause money demand to be less than money supply. Since the monetary authorities in Mexico are willing to buy or sell international reserves at a fixed price of 12.50 pesos per dollar, private citizens and/or business could determine the amount of high-powered money. In this case money demand is less than money supply; therefore planned money expenditures rise, with part of the increased expenditures appearing in the foreign goods and assets markets.

Mexicans may obtain reserve currencies from the Central Bank to pay for goods, services, and assets purchased outside Mexico. This process causes a decline in high-powered money, since member banks' reserves of currency are lowered when foreign reserves are purchased by the public. The fall in high-powered money is accompanied by the loss of assets in the form of foreign reserves. The purchase of foreign reserves by the public lowers high-powered money, and thereby generates a decline in the money stock. In this case a return to the previous equilibrium would imply a decline of high-powered money by 400 million pesos, and a decline of demand deposits (or of demand deposits plus currency) by 400 million pesos.

With the advent of flexible exchange rates another scenario may be developed. First, to facilitate the discussion, let us make the standard implicit, if not explicit, assumption that the elasticity of substitution between the Mexican peso and other currencies is zero. Now suppose that the authorities follow a truly flexible rate policy of never intervening, thereby targeting their reserve level at $\bar{R}$. This is tantamount to saying, momentarily, that Mexico may be treated as a closed economy.

Returning to our discussion of money creation, we can see the different effect of domestic credit creation on the system. Again assume that the supply of and demand for money are in equilibrium when the authorities initiate the increase in domestic credit. Ceteris paribus, the increase causes money demand to be less than supply. With equilibrium demand less than supply, planned expenditures rise; persons try to purchase goods, services, and bonds, some of which could be bought outside Mexico. As people go to exchange dealers to obtain necessary foreign currencies, they find that their demand for the currencies drives the exchange rate (pesos/dollars) up because the Bank of Mexico no longer satisfies their demand for international reserves. With the exchange rate appreciating, they try to purchase domestic goods. In a strict monetarist case of full employment and no money illusion, domestic prices are driven up until equilibrium between nominal money supply and money demand has been regained.

In the context of our fixed rate discussion, R does not move. Instead, equilibrium in demand for and supply of money is achieved internally with a higher level of prices and a higher (400 million pesos, in our example) level of money. In our subsequent discussion, when we describe what has taken place since 1954, one must bear in mind that the fixed exchange rate case is applicable.

Domestic Credit, Assets and Liabilities
of the Bank of Mexico

Let us begin the analysis of domestic credit by properly defining this concept for Mexico. If one defines $H = R + D$ from the balance sheet of Chapter 2, then domestic credit must be other assets minus other liabilities $(OA - OL)$. An examination of a balance sheet for the Bank of Mexico is useful at this point. Table 5.3 presents the balance sheet of the Central Bank of Mexico for December 31, 1973.

One may see from this balance sheet the magnitude of other assets and other liabilities. The largest liability of the Central Bank for 1973 is high-powered money and the largest asset is investments, most of which are held in government fixed-interest securities. Total assets minus foreign reserves equals other assets (OA), and total liabilities minus high-powered money (H) equals other liabilities (OL). Since $D = OA - OL$, the largest factor contributing to domestic credit in Mexico on December 31, 1973, was government fixed-interest securities. This high percentage of assets in government securities is a new phenomenon for Mexico since 1954, though it is similar to the present situation in the United States. On April 9, 1975, 79.2 percent of the assets of the Federal Reserve System were in the form of U.S. government securities.

The amount of assets held in government securities in 1973 was more than three times the amount held in foreign reserves, a new occurrence for Mexico. In 1957 the assets of the Central Bank were almost 60 percent foreign exchange, gold, and silver. Indeed, in 1957 the amount of government assets held (including short-term loans) was only 29.7 percent of the total foreign reserves held by the bank. As recently as 1967, international reserves and government security holdings were about equal. This fact will be very important in the later examination of domestic credit and its relationship to fiscal policy. Indeed, this earlier period, during which most of the sources of high-powered money were gold and foreign reserves, is similar to the early period of the Federal Reserve System (1920s-1940s). The early Federal Reserve System held more

TABLE 5.3

Assets and Liabilities of the Bank of Mexico, December 31, 1973
(million pesos)

Assets		
Foreign reserves		17,976
Bank cash		422
Investment in securities		
Government fixed-interest	59,197	
Other	1,457	
Total investment in securities		60,654
Loans		4,134
Other assets		6,510
Liabilities		
High-powered money		
Notes and coins	36,901	
Bank deposits	11,491	
Time deposits	26,715	
Total high-powered money		75,107
Other liabilities		
Treasury	1,747	
Business and individual	2,780	
Others	7,791	
Total other liabilities		12,318

Note: Assets = liabilities plus capital, surplus, and reserves of 2,271 million pesos.
Source: Statistics on the Mexican Economy (Mexico City: Nacional Financiera, 1974).

than 50 percent of the source of H (high-powered money) in gold and silver stocks or certificates.

Further analysis of the balance sheet for 1973 shows that high-powered money is by far the greatest liability of the Central Bank. Notes and coins in 1973 contributed 42 percent of the total liabilities, while in 1967 the figure was 62 percent and in 1957 around 60 percent. Indeed, the percentage of liabilities due to notes and coins remained virtually unchanged until 1972, when the amount of high-powered money began to grow rapidly. The year 1972 also witnessed a decline in the percentage contribution of the notes and coin category to total assets. In the early 1970s, the domestic increases in high-powered money came from deposits in new time accounts in the Central Bank.

These new time deposits were largely due to a conscious effort by the Central Bank to increase liquidity in the financial sector. It bought government securities in order to increase assets. These new funds were used to finance government expenditures, thereby entering the money supply and, ceteris paribus, causing a rise in high-powered money (a rise in bank reserves in the form of bank deposits and time deposits).

Mexican Domestic Credit Creation and the Bank Reserve Mechanism

There are several procedures by which the monetary authorities in Mexico can expand domestic credit. Referring to Table 5.3, one notes that any increase in other assets (OA) will increase domestic credit unless met by equal increases in other liabilities (OL). Historically OL has remained stable at 15 to 20 percent of total liabilities; OA has risen dramatically, and consequently has caused domestic credit (D) to rise sharply relative to high-powered money (H). Thus, to fully understand how domestic credit is increased, one should closely examine the experience of other assets in Mexico. A rise in OA may be accomplished through purchasing securities from either the government or the private sector. OA could increase by the making of private, government, or banking industry loans. Finally, OA may be enlarged by making direct loans to businesses and individuals.

As a matter of policy, the purchase of investment securities was used throughout 1954–75 to impact Mexican domestic credit. Dealings in securities should not be confused with the open market operations of the U.S. Federal Reserve System. The Central Bank did not attempt to function directly in an open market capacity, since there is no well-organized bond market, as there is in the United States. These purchases of securities were intended explicitly for the expansion of funds in the banking system and provision of liquidity for development or for public financing.

During the late 1950s investment in government securities fell at an annual rate of 6.24 percent, although the movements were erratic. Government security holdings continued to decline through 1963. From 1964 through 1972, however, they leaped by approximately 17 billion pesos and by 1968 were the largest single type of asset held. The stock of securities declined again (21.1 percent) during the 1970–71 credit tightening, then doubled in 1972. In 1973 government security holdings increased another 60 percent.

These data may be interpreted in the following manner. Under the public expenditure and deficit spending policy guidelines, the Mexican government did not rely mainly upon the Central Bank to finance increased government expenditures until the 1970s. A mechanism that shifted much of the responsibility for debt financing away from the Central Bank and to the private banking community was established, and the Central Bank was charged with providing funds for public investment by reallocating resources from the private to the public sector. As discussed, Mexico did not have a well-developed bond market, and thus the Treasury could not obtain large amounts of savings directly from the domestic private sector through issuance of government bonds. This differs dramatically from the American situation, where a well-developed market for U.S. Treasury issues exists. In the United States, the Federal Reserve acts as a banker for the Treasury, since these securities are sold directly in the financial markets.

The Central Bank chose not to expand the monetary base significantly through domestic credit creation. Therefore, given a policy of expanding the private and semiprivate financial sectors, the federal government could tap these expanding resources, using the Central Bank as an intermediary. Through the required reserve mechanism the bank found its answer to the open market operation for controlling the composition of high-powered money. The Central Bank and the financial authorities created a system of reserve requirements that would transfer funds from the private sector to the public sector. The Central Bank can raise these requirements or allow a greater percentage of reserves presently held to be in the form of government securities, and thus shift funds from the banking community to the authorities.

Though this method of debt financing does not cause increases in domestic credit, it affects the money supply through the money multiplier. During 1954–75 the use of the required reserve mechanism to finance public debt was common. Indeed, during the late 1960s and early 1970s the authorities frequently used their ability to set required reserves, changing them many times.

The frequent use of required reserve changes differs from that of the U.S. Federal Reserve System, where changes in reserve requirements were less common over the period (despite several changes in 1975). In the United States the required reserves are not held in the form of bonds, but as deposits in the Federal Reserve System. Further, the use of open market operations in the United States precludes the necessity for active use of the reserve requirement to control the money supply. The availability of a bond market allows transfers of savings from the private to the public sector without the coercion of the required reserve, as in Mexico.

The Mexican required reserve policy complemented the development policies of the period and worked well during the 1950s and 1960s. It did, however, create a dependence upon the financial sector for government financing, and required a growing financial sector to capture increasing amounts of savings from the public. Mort Gabriel notes that the financial sector grew at an annual rate (measured in assets) of 16.4 percent between 1946 and 1966.[2] As long as the financial sector expanded rapidly and domestic savings grew at a high rate, the transfer could be made at a rate sufficient to satisfy the needs of public expenditures.

During the 1950s and 1960s the required reserve mechanism was relied upon to finance government debt. Because of inadequate resources from the fiscal revenue structure, increased dependence was placed upon the reserve mechanism to supply treasury needs. The reserve mechanism was taxed each time an increased flow of funds was required to support greater public expenditure, or conditions worsened in the fiscal revenue structure. Each time the reserve requirements increased, there was a rise in the outstanding treasury bonds. This action reduced the possibility for use of the reserve requirement as a tool to control the money supply, and thwarted the ability of the authorities to use it to transfer funds from the private to the public sector. The Central Bank was earlier able to use this mechanism to finance public deficits, since public expenditure grew at a rate close to the growth in real income, and since the savings rate increased.

During 1972–75 several pressures were brought to bear on this mechanism. In 1970 and 1971 the authorities attempted to tighten credit in order to combat an expanding money supply. One tool used was the reserve requirement. It was increased to insure a fall in the money multiplier and to decrease the need for domestic credit creation, since more private capital could be diverted to the public sector. Though the effects of this policy were to keep domestic credit from growing at a rate less than the world rate of growth in the money supply and to lower the money multiplier, it did not significantly lower the rate of growth in the domestic money supply. The year 1971 witnessed a 7.76 percent increase in the growth of foreign reserves, scaled by the ratio of foreign reserves over high-powered money (that is, the growth in high-powered money due to reserves). One effect of the policy was to lower assets of the Central Bank held in the form of government fixed-interest assets and to increase international reserve holdings.

In 1972 expansionary fiscal policy was designed to counter the decline in the rate of real growth experienced in 1971. To finance the expansionary fiscal policy, the Central Bank was called upon to provide the necessary funds, which were not available from either the private financial sector or fiscal revenue policies. Combined with the drop in the real savings rate, the reserve requirement mechanism could not fully finance the new expenditures by the federal authorities. The inflexibility of this mechanism in 1972, combined with the inelastic nature of the fiscal revenue system, placed the responsibility for public finance upon the Central Bank, which increased its holdings of government debt more than twofold in 1972 and by another 60 percent in 1973. These increases led to a much greater growth in OA (as OL remained approximately the same) and, thus, to an expansion in domestic credit.

The new circumstances of 1972—recession and inflation—placed a strain upon the required reserve mechanism. The tool could no longer be depended upon to provide sufficient funds to meet the demands of the Treasury. Several factors, not the least of which was the world rate of inflation, contributed to the ineffectiveness of this tool by decreasing its versatility.

The rule associated with maintaining a slow growth in public expenditure was difficult to maintain in the 1970s, and the policy of tight money was fruitless because the world money supply was growing at a more rapid rate than was the goal of the Mexican authorities. With incipient world recession and now slower growth rates in Mexican real income, savings expanded at a slower rate. The expansion of the financial community and its general maturation meant that capturing increased financial resources for the central government was more difficult. To be specific, savings that previously were not channeled through the financial sector were becoming more difficult to capture as the total amount available outside the system was falling. Maturation of the financial system implies that savings outside the financial sector, such as those typical of a barter economy, or savings that would be held in kind rather than deposited in *financieras*, were diminishing. Finally, the inflexibility of the fiscal revenue structure began to bring greater pressure on the Central Bank to finance government deficits.

Direct Loans, Domestic Credit, and Sectoral Allocation

Expansion of direct loans to the government or the private sector was yet another mechanism by which the Central Bank could have helped finance government deficit. This type of loan was not used as a means of financing large amounts of public debt; indeed, it was used primarily to finance private-sector investment. The amount of outstanding loans to the federal government increased from less than 100 million pesos in 1954 to about 1.33 billion in 1966, and since that time it has hovered around 1 billion. The steady growth of this asset was a result of the monetary and fiscal policies of the late 1950s and early 1960s. During the 1970s, however, the Central Bank and the Treasury officials were more inclined to use fixed-interest securities as a mechanism to transfer funds to the Treasury.

Direct loans by the Central Bank were determined primarily by development criteria. A large percentage of the loans were to private industry and to individuals. Thus, they were not used for extending long-run credit to the public sector; most were expended largely to implement private development projects. The amount of the direct loans ranged from 413.8 million pesos in 1955 to 4,134.1 million pesos in 1973. The greatest expansion of direct loans occurred in 1963, when they amounted to 7,839.2 million pesos, approximately 80 percent of which were business and individual loans. Since business and individual loans played a large part in the creation of OA during 1954–64, it is evident that the Central Bank was active in promoting investment in particular sectors. In

TABLE 5.4

Selected Assets of the Central Bank of Mexico, Selected Years, 1954–73
(million pesos)

	1954	1956	1960	1964	1968	1972	1973
Business and individual loans, and investments							
Pesos	773.6	874.8	2,740.2	5,412.6	1,610.8	1,137.0	n.a.
Percent of total assets[a]	9.73	8.80	20.70	27.16	5.39	1.69	n.a.
Total private loans and investments							
Pesos	1,860.0	1,506.1	4,399.9	7,890.9	2,825.0	2,755.4	4,427.9[b]
Percent of total assets[a]	23.39	15.15	33.32	39.59	9.46	4.09	4.93[b]
Total public debt held by Central Bank							
Pesos	1,794.4	1,535.7	1,944.0	2,527.2	12,192.8	38,487.3	60,360.4[b]
Percent of total assets[a]	22.57	15.45	14.72	12.68	40.85	57.23	67.29[b]
Total private/total public	1.04	0.98	2.26	3.12	.231	.07	.07
Total assets	7,949.3	9,935.0	13,204.6	19,928.3	29,844.7	67,238.8	89,696.5

[a]Percentages do not sum to 100 because cash in banks and foreign exchange are considered part of total assets.
[b]Approximation
Note: n.a. = data not available.
Source: Statistics on the Mexican Economy (Mexico City: Nacional Financiera, 1974), pp. 229–38.

1965 the bank began to liquidate much of its direct business and individual loan portfolio and to shift the majority of its holdings to government securities.

With the inadequacies of fiscal revenues, a larger share of responsibility for financing public expenditure was placed on monetary policy. The reduced effectiveness of the reserve mechanism began to place pressure upon the Central Bank to finance new government expenditures directly, rather than indirectly. However, either loaning funds directly to the public and to the government or buying securities will have the same effect on OA and, therefore, on domestic credit creation. Thus, in the late 1950s and early 1960s domestic credit was generated to a greater extent directly from the Central Bank to the public in the form of loans and discounting, while in the late 1960s domestic credit creation was due primarily to government debt financing.

Table 5.4 indicates the trend in relative expansion of public and private assets held by the Central Bank during 1954–73. In addition, it illustrates the change in policy governing direct business and individual loans. As late as 1964, direct business and individual loans constituted 27.16 percent of total assets. A change in policy governing the bank's portfolio, however, allowed this type of asset to fall in both relative and nominal terms. In 1972 it contributed only 1.69 percent of the total assets.

One reason for deemphasis of the direct business and individual loan category in the late 1960s could be the ability of the private and semiprivate financial intermediaries to service private industry more completely; the Nacional Financiera, along with private *financieras*, had grown to such an extent that their assets were greater than those of the commercial banking system. In 1969 the total assets of *financieras* had grown to 48 percent of total assets of all financial intermediaries. Since *financieras* are involved in financing projects similar to those of interest to the Central Bank, such as energy and infrastructure development, it may be argued that the necessity of direct business and individual financing by the Central Bank is lessened. However, it is more likely that the increasingly pressured fiscal revenue generation system, along with the burdened required reserve mechanism, placed pressure upon the Central Bank to reduce credit creation in the private sector, a fortiori a reduction in direct loans to the private sector and increased credit to the public sector.

The dramatic rise in public sector financing is evident from Table 5.4. On December 31, 1954, 22.57 percent of the total assets of the Central Bank were in public assets, largely fixed-interest securities. Further, 23.39 percent of total assets were in the form of private securities and loans, divided almost evenly between loans and fixed-interest securities. After 1954, the bank consciously sought to reduce these assets while increasing its foreign reserve position and, with impetus generated by the 1954 devaluation, by early 1956 held only 15.45 percent of its assets portfolio in public assets such as treasury securities and direct government loans, while only 15.15 percent was in private assets. The remainder consisted of cash, foreign exchange, or fixed assets. By 1964 the public debt was further reduced to 12.68 percent. By 1968, however, the percentage of public assets held had more than doubled from 1964, and by 1973 public assets had risen to constitute 67.29 percent of the Central Bank portfolio.

A summary of the change in the ratio of private to public assets is presented in the seventh row of Table 5.4. The ratio was approximately 1 until the late 1950s. Because of growing Central Bank involvement in private sector investments, the ratio rose to 2.26 in 1960 and 3.12 in 1964. In 1968 the ratio had fallen drastically to .231 and, with the increased demands upon the bank for public investment funding, plunged to .07 in 1972 and 1973.

These ratios reflect the goals of monetary and fiscal policy during the period. As increased domestic credit creation was being demanded by the public (if domestic credit creation was to keep pace with foreign reserves as a contribution to high-powered money), the "other assets" category had to increase. In retrospect, OA (and therefore D) increased at a rate much greater than that of foreign reserves. The ratios show that until the late 1960s, growth in domestic credit was not a result of demands for government financing. Indeed, the portion of the portfolio of Central Bank assets pertaining to the private sector indicates the effectiveness of the alternative sources of government revenue—taxation, foreign borrowing, and the mechanism for generating required reserve revenue. The emphasis of the Central Bank could be on private sector allocation of resources. Since the bank was also interested in sectoral allocation of credit, the ability to expand domestic credit directly through the private sector, in theory, produced the ability to control sectoral as well as public-to-private domestic credit allocation (the ramifications of sectoral allocation are discussed in detail in Chapter 6).

While the ratio of private to public assets fell during the late 1960s, this period witnessed a movement in emphasis from private sector allocation to public sector financing. Fixed-interest government securities became more important as an asset to the Central Bank. The private-to-public asset ratio of .07 for 1973 indicates that policy changes placed a greater responsibility for public debt financing upon the Central Bank. The reasons for this change in policy are not arbitrary, but are a consequence of earlier development and monetary policies, as well as of world movements in prices and money. An examination of the late 1960s and early 1970s may illuminate the policy changes.

Domestic Credit Creation and Demands of the Early 1970s

During the time that the rate of growth in the world money supply and price levels was relatively low, the rate of growth in domestic credit, adjusted by the ratio of domestic credit to high-powered money, grew at a rate similar to that of real income. Given the growth rate in world money supply, the price level, and the Mexican financial sector, the relatively slow growth of domestic credit was consistent with policy prescriptions of the monetary approach to balance of payments required to maintain a positive balance of payments. During 1969, 1970, and 1971 the Central Bank attempted to lower the growth rate of money supply by restricting domestic credit creation. To counter the slow expansion of domestic money stock, large amounts of foreign reserves entered Mexico; and in 1971 the growth rate of foreign reserves multiplied by foreign reserves over high-powered money was almost twice the growth rate in domestic credit multiplied by domestic credit over high-powered money. The monetary approach to balance of payments would predict that foreign exchange reserves would flow in if domestically supplied money increased at a rate less than money demand. The implication of the restrictive monetary policy of 1969, 1970, and 1971 is clear: slow growth in domestic credit, along with the rapid growth in money demand, generated substantial reserve inflow. The reserve inflows during 1969, 1970, and 1971 (at a time when the balance of trade was worsening) were the direct result of a demand for foreign exchange reserves to maintain the equilibrium in money supply and demand at the same time that monetary authorities were attempting to slow the growth in the money supply.

It would appear, as has been argued here, that the money stock was beyond the control of the Bank of Mexico during this period. The direct effect of credit restriction was offset by unanticipated—though theoretically expected on the basis of monetary approach theories—foreign reserve inflows (that is, foreign exchange inflows equilibrated the demand for and supply of money).

During most of 1954–75 the ratio of private to public assets in the Central Bank portfolio was largely at the discretion of the monetary authorities. Since increased public expenditures were demanded for the development program, pressure was placed upon the bank to use the required reserve mechanism. Further, as argued in Chapter 3, import-substitution policies lessened the effectiveness of the fiscal revenue generating mechanism. Therefore, the government was inclined to use direct monetary policy to finance government debt. With the lessened effectiveness of the required reserve mechanism in the 1960s and 1970s, the Central Bank had little choice but to initiate purchases of government securities. It therefore had either to lower its private sector assets or to face increasing amounts of domestic credit creation. One effect of development and fiscal policies of the 1950s and 1960s, therefore, was to reduce the capacity of the Central Bank to control its outlets for domestic credit creation.

Though the bank did select among its money creation "outlets" (including the federal government, private and semiprivate banking, and private business and individuals) in the late 1950s and 1960s, the selection of such outlets during the 1970s was academic at best. In short, the effects of earlier policy (including fiscal revenue inelasticity resulting from import-substitution policy, the full utilization of the required reserve mechanism, and the decline in growth of the financial sector) effectively restricted policy option to government financing.

In our examination of domestic credit creation, the sources and channels of its creation have been investigated. An alternative method of domestic credit creation analysis concentrates upon the factors that cause its creation. This alternative approach to domestic credit analysis can better place the required reserve ratio mechanism and fiscal revenue sources of government finance in proper perspective as they relate to domestic credit.

An Alternative Elaboration of Domestic Credit

The alternative approach to domestic credit creation analysis is based upon the Borts-Hanson definition of domestic credit.[3] They define ΔD as $\Delta D = (Y_g - t - i_b)$, where the sources of government funds (including taxes t and government debt i_b) are subtracted from government expenditures (Y_g). The remainder (ΔD) must be domestically created credit—that is, money used to finance a government deficit. Clearly, a government surplus would be associated with a negative D (given that i_b is not negative—that is, no debt retirement).

The model is based upon a combined Treasury and Central Bank balance sheet. For Mexico, domestic credit may be created by the Central Bank's loaning directly to businesses and individuals as well as its using government and private banking channels. Therefore, any action by the Central Bank to make direct loans must be entered into the calculation of Y_g.

Domestic credit may be used by the monetary authorities to control the money supply in the short run, although the control will be fully offset by foreign reserve inflow or outflow in the long run. Since $\Delta D = (Y_g - t - i_b)$, the control rests in determining the amount of the government deficit to be monetized, either directly or indirectly. As noted earlier, the policy of Mexican authorities since 1954 has been to keep monetary expansion at a rate permitting maintenance of a fixed exchange rate. To this end they have attempted to regulate ΔD so as to hold inflation at a level commensurate with the world rate. Therefore, deficit financing has been handled largely through domestic and foreign borrowing via the required reserve mechanism and bond sales, primarily in the U.S. markets.

Government Borrowing

An increase in government borrowing (i_b) reduces ΔH. Such borrowing is financed chiefly through the legislative requirement that commercial banks and *financieras* must hold a specified percentage of their asset portfolio in public debt. As of December 31, 1969, the public sector total debt was 92,874,000 pesos, with approximately 47.6 percent financed outside Mexico and 52.4 percent funded internally.

The Central Bank has no open market committee to control the monetary base through purchases and sales of government securities. The compulsory deposit, required reserve mechanism laws of 1941, 1949, and 1958 allow it an alternative to the open market mechanism. A target rate of deposit growth may be established by the Central Bank for individual commercial banks. Those that cannot attract reserves sufficient to meet the prescribed annual rate of increase in deposits may borrow reserves from the Central Bank, thus allowing commercial banks that are below the target rate to borrow funds. At the same time the Central Bank disallows loans to those commercial banks whose deposit growth exceeds the target.

Further, the Central Bank exercises limited control over the placement of public debt instruments in commercial banks through a discount window. Although published discount rates are established, the actual rate for any specific commercial paper loan is left to the discretion of the Central Bank. Thus, through a variable discount rate it can influence the placement of the discount window that allocates credit to particular industries by means of the discretionary discount rate policy. The window also provides support for commercial banks that experience short-term losses of deposits, thus preventing, in some cases, commercial bank failure. The discount window permits the Central Bank not only to be the lender of last resort but also to serve as a vehicle to control the monetary base in the short run. In addition it allows the bank to maintain some control over domestically financed government borrowing, and greater control over credit allocation.

In addition to the compulsory deposit and discount window tools, the bank can influence the composition of financial intermediary assets by assisting in the placement of new government debt—and, therefore, domestic credit and the money stock. Federal legislation has given power to the Central Bank to influence the asset portfolios of financial institutions as adviser and as enforcer of banking laws.

As we have discussed, the majority of government fixed-interest securities held by the public were placed with financial intermediaries. However, the government did take advantage of the securities market directly. Over the period, a market for fixed-interest securities, which were traded at par through repurchase agreements, began to develop. However, the type of market development precluded the necessity to form a secondary market, such as exists in the United States. For example, a tax-year maturity bond that yielded a 9 percent rate of return could be redeemed at par any time during a ten-year period. Thus, if the interest rate rose, one would be able to redeem the bond with no capital loss. During the 1950s this market developed rapidly and was a major vehicle by which the financial community (and in turn the government) could mobilize domestic resources. John Thompson notes that one of the most important factors contributing to the development of this sector was the stability of prices and the exchange rate.

The essential condition for the growth of the market in peso-denominated fixed-interest securities was an atmosphere of stability and the public confidence that relative yields on alternative assets would remain stable or at least predictable, instead of changing abruptly as a result of general price increases and devaluation. The authorities, especially the Bank of Mexico, assigned an important role to expectations and the need to develop confidence on the part of the public in the value of money, financial assets, and the soundness of institutions. In the thinking of the authorities, the country's history of inflation and financial crises, and large devaluations had made the Mexican public wary of holding domestic financial assets and therefore the Mexican financial system vulnerable to panic and capital flight. Accordingly, official policy sought in many ways not merely to create incentives for the development of financial markets but also to convince the public that stability-oriented policies were a permanent feature of official policy rather than a transient policy of a single Administration.[4]

Within this atmosphere the public sector took advantage of the financial market's growth to place its issues directly into the hands of the public, although the main center of financing remained the financial community.

In summary, one may for the most part relate publicly held government debt to the following variables: reserve requirement, Central Bank discount policy, asset structure and policy of financial institutions, compulsory discount tool, and the growth of the securities market. A change in any of these variables will influence H. Therefore, in the short run the Central Bank may increase i_b, thereby lowering ΔD and, ceteris paribus, ultimately reduce high-powered money. Domestic government borrowing and the money supply are, therefore, negatively related. On the other hand, liquidation of debt or purchase of outstanding notes by the Mexican government will be positively related to the money supply. One concludes, therefore, that the Mexican Central Bank has tools available similar to those of the U.S. Federal Reserve System that may be used to adjust the money stock in the short run. To the extent that the exercise of these tools by monetary authorities is not offset by reserve flows, the use of these controls will effect a change in H.*

---

*It should be noted that the Mexican government has actively promoted private borrowing. The process is carried out by the Central Bank's actively providing (along with political and economic stability) incentive to private banks and *financieras* to obtain foreign deposits. One incentive is the curtailing of liquidity for the private sector while simultaneously providing a fiscal climate for increased private investment. Other legislative acts have provided a climate that protects investors' interests through a set of tax incentives, guarantees on deposits, and complete banker-client discretion. Gilberto Escobedo suggested

Since nongovernment foreign borrowing is used as the adjustment mechanism for changing domestic credit (and, implicitly, domestic borrowing), the supply of money = money demand relationship controls the level of nongovernment foreign borrowing. Assume that the Central Bank raises borrowing, thereby generating a growth in the money supply less than the growth in money demand. With $gM^d > gM^s$ the financial community seeks outside funds. Foreign exchange reserves rise as a result of increased nongovernment foreign borrowing, thus causing a positive change in high-powered money and increasing the money supply until equilibrium is reestablished. To the extent that movement in borrowing is fully anticipated, nongovernment foreign borrowing will fully offset it and equilibrium will be maintained as persons purchase foreign exchange.

The Alternative Model and Tax Policy

The ability of the fiscal authorities to increase the level of tax revenues (t) is critical to controlling ΔD. If the tax system is relatively income-elastic, it should provide a level of t sufficient to meet government expenditures. If the tax system is relatively income-inelastic, as income increases (as demand for public services rises), one encounters a situation where t is at a level well below that required to meet government expenditures. We have shown that such is the situation Mexico now faces.

The tax generating structure has been extremely important to the development of the Mexican financial structure. One reason that the Central Bank must resort to monetary policy in financing government debt is that the government has been unable to significantly increase revenues from fiscal sources. Since domestic credit is negatively related to fiscal revenue, much of the Central Bank's effectiveness in using domestic credit as a policy tool (rather than as a variable responding largely to government demands for funds) depends upon the responsiveness of fiscal revenue to income change. The structure, however, is not very elastic with respect to income. Indeed, government expenditures in 1954 were financed almost completely by revenues from fiscal resources. In 1973 fiscal revenues amounted to only 67 percent of total government revenue receipts, non-Central Bank borrowing making up the rest. However, total revenues from borrowing and fiscal resources were below public expenditures. The remaining deficit, therefore, was monetized by Central Bank purchases of government securities and direct government loans.

---

to the author that these incentives, as well as free convertibility and a stable exchange rate, have been extremely important in moving savings into the financial community and then, through the reserve requirements, in financing government deficit. However, the instability of the 1970s, culminating in the 1976 devaluation, of course had the opposite effect.

Government Expenditures

To the extent that t and i_b do not offset Y_g (government expenditures), the latter is a factor in determining domestic credit. Although the government may clearly use its expenditures as a control factor for high-powered money creation, its importance as a policy instrument is not analyzed in this study except for the following tautology: Any increase in government expenditures must be offset by t or by domestically financed government borrowing. Otherwise, domestic credit will increase, since all $Y_g > (t + i_b)$ must be met by the Central Bank's generation of funds (domestic credit) to fill the gap.

In summary, this definitional approach to analyzing domestic credit creation is specifically aimed at deriving the different policy alternatives open to the authorities. All four variables in the identity

$$\Delta D = Y_g - t - i_b$$

can be considered policy variables to some extent. We have shown that tax revenues have lagged behind expenditures over most of the period since 1954. Thus, the policy variable alternatives open to the authorities to finance the government expenditures were mainly i_b and/or ΔD.

Financial development and expansion enabled the authorities, through various mechanisms, to mobilize these previously uncaptured savings for public investment. The authorities, in essence, depended upon the financial sector to absorb greater amounts of government debt. The growth in i_b helped neutralize the widening gap between expenditures and taxes. However, when the growth in i_b was not sufficient to finance the widening disparity between expenditures and taxes, domestic credit creation had to compensate for the residual. During the 1970s the authorities were faced with a policy decision. Since $(i_b + t)$ could not offset expenditures (Y_g), it was necessary to expand domestic credit.

The Money Multiplier

The second variable that can be influenced by the monetary authorities is the money multiplier. To further analyze the multiplier and its relevance for Mexico, we shall expand upon the derivation outlined in Chapter 2.

One may postulate, on the basis of a fractional reserve system for commercial banks, the balance sheet relationship

---

In the presentation of the money supply process in Mexico, notation will follow, where possible, that of Albert Burger, *The Money Supply Process* (Belmont, Calif.: Wadsworth, 1971).

$$D^P = \bar{R} + E$$

where

D^P = demand deposits
$\bar{R}$ = bank reserves
E = earning assets

Thus, $D^P/\bar{R} = 1 + (E/\bar{R})$. Let $r = \bar{R}/D^P$ where r = the reserve ratio. Thus, given a fractional reserve system, the banking system may create a money stock equivalent to the amount of reserves times the multiplier, $(1/r)$. Since banks must hold required reserves by law, total reserves may be divided into two parts: required and excess. Let r^d represent the legal reserve ratio, and e the ratio of excess reserves (reserves held above those legally required) to deposits. Therefore,

$$r = r^d + e \quad \text{and} \quad 1/r = 1/(r^d + e)$$

where r is the bank reserve ratio.

Two determinants of the money multiplier are, thus, the required reserve ratio established by legislation and the Central Bank, and the portfolio desires of the banking community. The manner in which individuals desire to allocate their holdings of money (currency or demand deposits) is expressed in the currency-deposit ratio, K, where $K = C^P/D^P$, C^P = the coin and currency held by the public, and D^P = the deposits held by the public. The reserve ratio, as a result, gives an incomplete picture of the multiplier effect of a movement in foreign reserves (or domestic credit) on money creation. Adding K to the equation, the money multiplier (a) is

$$a = \frac{1 + K}{(r^d + e) + K}$$

Further,

$$M_1 = \frac{1 + K}{(r^d + e) + K} \cdot H$$

where M_1 includes coin and currency in circulation plus noninterest-bearing deposits. See Figures 5.1 and 5.2 for historical movements in money and its components.

High-powered or base money (H) may be defined by identifying its sources. H is an asset of the financial sector that is supplied by the Central Bank and the Treasury. In Mexico these assets are determined by the balance sheet of the

Central Bank. That is, high-powered money may be defined as

$$H = C^p + \bar{R}$$

where

    C^p = the coin and currency held by the public
    $\bar{R}$ = total Central Bank reserves

The sources of the monetary base (H) are the Central Bank's holdings of Mexican government debt, the gold and foreign currency position, currency and float outstanding minus government deposits at the Central Bank, government cash balances, and private bank and *financiera* balances at the Central Bank. Many of the assets of development institutions in Mexico are obtained through foreign loans that are converted to pesos. Thus their effect on the base is captured under foreign reserves, since the net change in bank reserves is positively related to the deposit of the foreign reserves with the Central Bank.

FIGURE 5.1

Demand Deposits, Currency, and M_1, Mexico, 1954–73

Source: Compiled by the author.

FIGURE 5.2

Demand Deposits, Currency, and Bank Reserves, Mexico, 1954–73

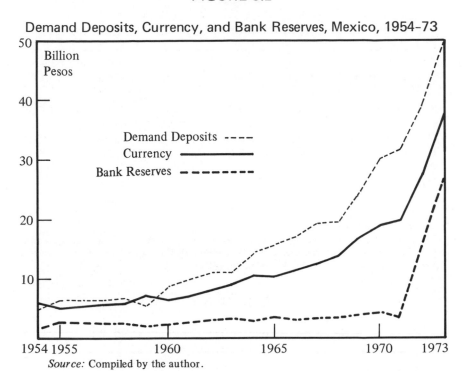

Source: Compiled by the author.

In the framework of this paper D is considered a policy variable; $\bar{R}$ is determined by the public's portfolio decisions, ceteris paribus; r^d is determined by the financial intermediaries; and K is a public-controlled variable. Table 5.5 reports the movements in the various determinants of the money supply where $r = r^d + e$. Consistently the largest contributors to the growth in the money stock have been increases in domestic credit and increases in foreign reserve holdings.

Foreign reserves work through high-powered money to change the money supply. As indicated earlier, changing $\bar{R}$ or ΔD will create movements in H that can effect a change in the money supply through the multiplier process.

Since money supply = a · H, changing the money multiplier, a, will also affect M_1. Recalling that

$$a = \frac{1 + K}{(r^d + e) + K}$$

government may change M_1 through r^d. The public determines K by the ratio of currency to demand deposits that it wishes to hold, while banks determine e in a

TABLE 5.5

Periodic Movements in the Money Stock and Its Determinants

Variable	Value 1954	Value 1960	1960	1973	Percent Change 1954–60	Percent Change 1954–73
K	1.110	0.874	0.713	0.748	−21.26	−32.68
r	0.419	0.283	0.244	0.574	−32.46	38.02
H	6.19B	10.43B	18.78B	75.21B	68.46	1,115.00
D	3.58B	4.90B	11.73B	58.26B	36.76	1,527.30
R	2.61B	5.53B	7.05B	16.95B	111.87	549.42
M_1	8.72B	16.89B	32.75B	79.87B	93.69	795.40

B = billion pesos.

Sources: Statistics on the Mexican Economy, (Mexico City: Nacional Financiera, 1974); *International Financial Statistics*, (Washington, D.C.: International Monetary Fund); *Informe Anual*, (Mexico City: Bank of Mexico, 1974).

FIGURE 5.3

Currency-to-Deposit Ratio, Mexico, 1954–73

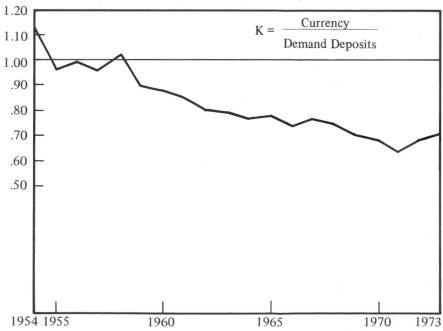

$$K = \frac{\text{Currency}}{\text{Demand Deposits}}$$

Source: Compiled by the author.

similar manner. (See Figure 5.3 for the historical movements of K in Mexico since 1954.) That is, the banking community may hold excess reserves, depending upon the expectations of future developments in the economy. Those reserves may be high if the banking community anticipates increases in r^d, or if faith in the Central Bank's handling of financial matters diminishes. Many factors, such as day-to-day demands for funds, will determine how the bank decides to hold its assets—in loans or in excess reserves.

Factors Influencing the Currency-to-Deposit Ratio

Several factors impact composition of the public's portfolio, and therefore influence K. The public will determine the form in which it desires to hold money balances (currency or demand deposits) on the basis of factors that are also instrumental in adjusting its wealth portfolio. First, confidence in the banking community can lower the K ratio, while instability, either political or economic, will raise it. Second, availability of banking services and the size of associated costs may alter the ratio, ceteris paribus. Third, as the Mexican financial community expands services to outer areas, one would expect the currency-to-deposit ratio to fall as a result of the availability of previously unavailable resources. Fourth, confidence in the countryside about financial services should make deposit banking more widely acceptable, and thereby lower the currency-to-deposit ratio. Fifth, seasonal factors and the level of economic activity may act to alter the ratio.

Figure 5.3 shows the historical trend of the currency-to-deposit ratio in Mexico, and graphically illustrates that the public has altered its balances over time from currency to demand deposits. The downward trend in K in 1954–73 is undoubtedly the result of a number of the factors listed above. The historical record of the currency-to-deposit ratio indicates the increased sophistication of the Mexican financial community. In 1954, K was greater than 1, while by 1971 the ratio had fallen by approximately 40 percent (see Figure 5.3). Some of the more important specific factors influencing the decline in K are the following. First, the Mexican financial community extended its services during the period, enabling even the most remote areas to take advantage of banking services. Second, the educational level (financial as well as academic) of the population advanced. Third, stable economic growth was characteristic of the. period. Fourth, relative political stability added to public confidence in the financial community.

Variations in the downward trend of K in Figure 5.3 are also of interest. In 1955, K fell below 1. However, this was short-lived, for it rose above 1 in 1958. Possibly the higher level of K during the 1958 period reflects public awareness of economic slowdown and decreased economic stability. The trend in K after 1958 was downward through 1971, with only slight fluctuations that mirrored minor movements in the business cycle. As anticipated, the trend after 1971 has been upward, with an increased internal inflation rate and growing domestic, as well as world, economic instability. On net, however, the trend in K has clearly been downward over the entire period.

The movement of K in Mexico can be compared with that in the United States. After World War II the K ratio for the United States declined until 1955, then remained steady at approximately .258 through 1962. The K ratio rose to .292 in 1969, and in 1972 it was .282. Indeed, in absolute terms the Mexican K ratio has been about three times that of the United States for much of the post-1954 period. This information gives more credence to the hypothesis that the fall in the Mexican K was due in some degree to the maturation of the financial sector.

Reserve-to-Deposit Ratio

The total reserve-to-deposit ratio (r), also critical in the determination of money supply, is to an extent under the control of the individual commercial banks through e. Legal reserve requirements, however, are considered the most important policy instrument of monetary authorities; and all financial institutions except mortgage companies hold required reserves at the Central Bank. The required ratio for commercial banks differs, depending upon location and type of deposit. Reserve requirements of financial institutions are such that the Mexican Central Bank can control, to a degree, the amount of resources that must be invested in various official government securities. Thus it has some control over total reserves ($r^d + e$). The Central Bank may also use the reserve requirements of financial institutions to allocate funds for government securities that affect i_b. The range of r for commercial banks will vary, depending upon the amount of excess reserves held by the commercial banks. In general, one may expect r to increase during recession and to contract during periods of expansion.

Figure 5.4 shows the movement in r from 1954 through 1973. As anticipated, bank reserves and the money supply show a high degree of correlation. Since

$$a = \frac{1 + K}{(r^d + e) + K}, \quad \partial a/\partial r^d < 0, \quad \partial a/\partial e < 0, \quad \partial a/\partial K < 0$$

then

$$\partial M_1/\partial r^d < 0, \quad \partial M_1/\partial e < 0, \quad \partial M_1/\partial K < 0$$

Clearly, an increase in r^d or e will lead to a decline in the money supply, given that H and K are constant. The effect of the public portfolio decision is measured in the movement of the currency-to-deposit ratio. An increase in K will

FIGURE 5.4

Bank Reserves-to-Deposit Ratio, Mexico, 1954-73

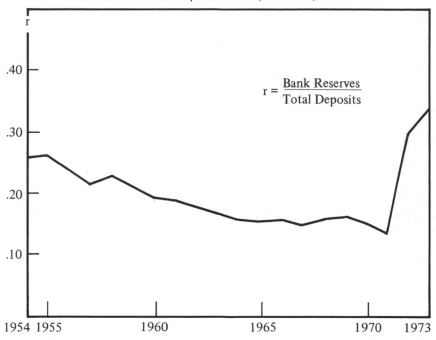

$$r = \frac{\text{Bank Reserves}}{\text{Total Deposits}}$$

Source: Compiled by the author.

have a negative effect on M_1. As noted earlier and demonstrated in Figure 5.3, the Mexican K moved from $K > 1$ to $K < 1$ during 1954-73. In 1954 and 1958, $K > 1$, with the remaining years showing $K < 1$. Thus, for most of the period of this study, the movement in K implied an increase in the money supply.

Referring to Figure 5.5, one notes the regularity of movements between Central Bank reserves, demand deposits, and the money supply. The movements of reserves closely parallel changes in the other money and in demand deposits. It is apparent that though the swings differ slightly in magnitude, the largest appears to be, as one would anticipate, bank reserves (a component of high-powered money). The period of relative stability in the money multiplier (1956-70) showed very little deviation in the tracks of the three. During 1971 and 1972, however, large increases in reserves, combined with a dramatic increase in the money multiplier, yielded a sharp increase in M_1 and demand deposits—but with much less relative increase than in the bank reserves. This result is consistent with our earlier discussion of monetary policy and domestic credit creation in connection with strong money demand in 1971, 1972, and 1973.

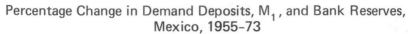

FIGURE 5.5

Percentage Change in Demand Deposits, M_1, and Bank Reserves, Mexico, 1955–73

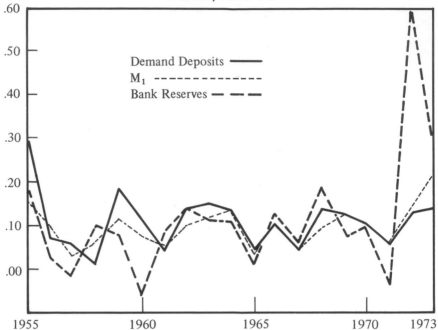

Source: Compiled by the author.

In conclusion, one may specify three important factors affecting the money multiplier: legal reserve requirements as determined by government legislation, the commercial bank decision on reserve balances, and the public portfolio decisions with respect to K. All of these effects have been important in Mexico since 1954. The K and r ratios fell for most of the period, having a slightly positive effect on the multiplier. The variable r fell despite continued increases in legislated r^d. This implied a fall in the factor e as banks became more confident of their financial positions. The public portfolio decisions concerning K were rational and reflected the growing acceptance of the financial sector and economic stability.

INTERNATIONAL VARIABLES

Since prices and interest rates are determined in the world goods and capital markets, respectively, an analysis of the impact (or lack thereof) of government policy upon these variables must begin by examining the empirical evidence.

That of Chapter 3 showed that for most of the period, the rate of change in prices in Mexico did not differ significantly from that of the United States on either a quarterly or an annual basis. In short, the rate of inflation can be exogenously determined for Mexico. The empirical evidence in Chapter 3 is fairly consistent with the assumption that interest rates are also determined in world markets; however, knowledge of Mexico's capital market suggests that the interest rates do tend to be less than flexible in response to market conditions. Thus prices and interest rates in Mexico and the United States are simultaneously determined in unified goods and bonds markets. Though both of these assumptions are based on theoretical foundations, they were empirically well-founded for most of the period prior to 1974 and 1975. One may appeal to international price arbitrage of goods and services as well as bonds to predict integration of world markets. An investigation of the implications of these assumptions based upon the empirical findings of Chapter 3 follows.

Prices and the Mexican Devaluation of 1954

Suppose that Mexico devalued the peso from a position of purchasing power parity (equilibrium prices are set by world conditions). One would then expect a readjustment of prices in Mexico vis-a-vis the United States. In April 1954, devaluation moved the exchange rate of the peso from 8.65 to 12.50 pesos per dollar. Simultaneously Mexico experienced a 5 percent inflation, following a 1.8 percent deflation in 1953. In 1955, while readjustment was continuing, the inflation rate was approximately 15 percent. In the United States the inflation rate was .69, .46, and .43 percent for 1953, 1954, and 1955, respectively. It is therefore clear that following the 1954 devaluation of the peso, Mexico experienced price increases at a rate much greater than that in the United States over a short period.

The Mexican rate of inflation then moved on a level consistent with the U.S. rate (see Figure 5.6). Indeed, the long-run trend of the U.S. and Mexican rates of inflation appear to be the same. As shown in Chapter 3, the rate of inflation in Mexico (π_m), regressed against the rate of inflation in the United States (π_{us}) for 1954-73, yielded an R^2 of only .01 and an insignificant F-level. The 1956-73 annual regression results were

$$\pi_m = 1.747 + .9280\pi_{us}$$
$$(1.414)\,(2.509)$$

$$R^2 = .282$$
$$F = 6.298$$
$$DW = 1.238$$

FIGURE 5.6

Consumer Price Indexes, United States and Mexico, 1954–74
(1963 = 100)

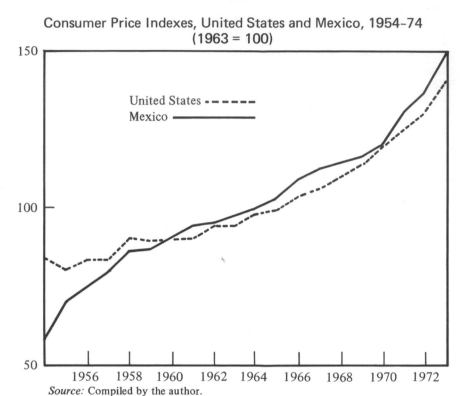

Source: Compiled by the author.

These results support the unified goods market hypothesis. The long-run tendency for prices of countries that maintain fixed exchange rates is to move at the same rates, due either to actual price arbitrage or to the expectations of price arbitrage.

With the devaluation in 1954 three goals of monetary policy were adopted. First, the primary function of the monetary authority was to maintain a fixed exchange rate. Second, the monetary authority was to finance government spending in a noninflationary manner. That is, the financial authorities were to find mechanisms of financing government expenditure that would not create excessive amounts of domestic credit. Third, monetary policy was to increase relative growth in those sectors of the economy viewed as strategic in maximizing economic growth. The first two goals were particularly geared to price stability.

The second goal of monetary policy is a result of the 1945–50 experience, when deficit spending by the Mexican government was financed by money creation. The use of the Central Bank to finance government deficit through domestic credit creation led to outflows of foreign reserves because domestic credit was increasing at a rate greater than money demand. The increases in the price indexes for 1952 and 1953 were mild, however, with an overall increase of about 1 percent. They followed a 9 percent increase in 1949 and a 20 percent devaluation of the peso vis-a-vis the dollar; a 10 percent rate of inflation in 1950; and a 25 percent rate of inflation in 1951 after the 1950 devaluation from 4.89 pesos to 8.64 per dollar. It is interesting to note that with the maintenance of a fixed exchange rate during 1951, 1952, and 1953, Mexico experienced a slow rate of inflation even though the rate of expansion of domestic credit creation was increasing—reserves flowed out. This is exactly what the monetary approach to the balance-of-payments model would suggest. Three goals of monetary policy were designed to eliminate this problem and promote economic development.*

Prices and Mexican Monetary Policy

The first two goals were designed to stabilize the cycle of devaluation and inflation, while the third was utilized to support development policy targets. During the late 1950s and 1960s the goals of monetary policy were consistent with the maintenance of a fixed exchange rate, a positive or zero balance of payments, a slow growth in the money stock similar to or slightly greater than the rate of real growth, and a slow rate of growth in the price level. During the 1950s and the 1960s there was no conflict between slow rates of inflation and zero balance of payments. However, during the early 1970s, officials concluded that inflation in Mexico could be slowed through a number of different channels.

Mexican monetary policy was designed to restrict the money supply and thereby reduce demand for goods and services (and, ultimately, the rate of inflation). The authorities attempted to restrict the money supply by lowering the money multiplier in 1971, 1972, and 1973. The growth in domestic credit, scaled by domestic credit over high-powered money, increased by only 3.33 percent in 1970 and 4.69 percent in 1971. The result of the domestic policy was an inflow of foreign reserves that increased high-powered money, thus insuring equilibrium of money supply and money demand. In 1972 the authorities

---

*The definition of the aim of the three goals of monetary policy follows from discussion between individuals of the Central Bank of Mexico and this author. For further insights see Arturo Ruíz Equihua and Leopoldo Solis, "Aspectos generales de los instrumentos de política monetaria y crediticia en México," unpublished working paper, Centro de Estudios Monetarios Latinamericanos, IX Reunión Operativa, Buenos Aires, November 1968; and Gilberto Escobedo, "Ahorro y desarrallo económico," Bank of Mexico working paper, 1975.

rapidly expanded domestic credit (federal fiscal policy) while attempting to slow growth in the money supply by lowering the money multiplier. The inability of monetary policy to control prices has led to other fiscal measures, such as price controls on selected items and price freezes similar to those administered in the United States.

If one views the Mexican experience as that of a small country on fixed exchange rates, the movements in the price level since the mid-1950s are all consistent, not with particular government policies but with Mexico's position in the world goods market. Indeed, it should be asked whether policies were consistent with the growth in world prices, not whether prices responded to policies. During 1954–69 prices and policy were consistent. In the early 1970s policy was intended to lower growth in prices, but prices continued to inflate at the world rate. The rate of inflation for 1970, 1971, and 1972 was a total of 16.02 percent in Mexico, while in the United States it was 14.14 percent. Referring to the empirical section, it is apparent that one cannot reject the null hypothesis of a unified goods market. The quarterly analysis strongly supports the hypothesis that inflation rates between the United States and Mexico did not significantly differ over this period. (See Tables 3.2–3.4. Also see Chapter 6 for a further analysis of general monetary policy during 1970–74.)

The mid-1970s presented a totally different price picture. We have demonstrated that the Mexican inflation rate could not be shown to have deviated significantly from an equilibrium path during the early 1970s. However, the controls put into effect during the early 1970s and the export subsidies used to keep prices of traded goods in line with those of the rest of the world eventually led to a situation that allowed growth of the Mexican Consumer Price Index to dramatically diverge from that of the United States in late 1974, 1975, and early 1976. Since the devaluation of the peso took place on September 1, 1976, one cannot determine whether the discrepancy in inflation rates because of these market disruptions will cease. Certainly the rapid increase in prices following the devaluation suggests that Mexicans are aware of the international prices vis-a-vis Mexican prices and adjust accordingly.

Interest Rates in Mexico

Some have argued that the interest rate differential is a major factor contributing to Mexican success in attracting foreign capital and in generating capital account surpluses. Clark Reynolds, R. W. Goldsmith, and Robert Bennett suggest that these differentials in interest rates between Mexico and other countries have been an important policy tool for the Central Bank of Mexico, while other economists imply that these differentials are set in the marketplace and reflect the difference in risk between Mexican and world (U.S.) securities.[5] We would contend that they are a result of market phenomena and not of active Central Bank policy, and represent responses of bank policy to market considerations.

The nominal levels of interest rates in Mexico can, and do, differ from the nominal rates for similar types of securities in the United States, Europe, or Japan. A casual examination of Figures 3.1 and 3.2 shows that Mexican and United States composite rates are different for securities of similar maturity. ANOVA tests show that in Mexico, the Netherlands, France, Belgium, Germany, and Canada the levels of the long-term rate of interest are different. There is no question that countries may have different levels of interest rate for similar securities.

Though levels of interest rates in Mexico have differed from those of the five other countries mentioned (through liquidity premiums or transaction costs associated with the individual country's security), an ANOVA test shows that the mean percentage change of the nominal interest rate was not different. The individual country has not arbitrarily increased or decreased the nominal rate of interest relative to the world rate of interest (and perhaps cannot do so). While the F-level for ANOVA tests (using Mexico and the United States) for the period (quarterly data) 1960–72 was 1,135.0 when levels were analyzed, the F-level was only .978 when percentage changes were compared. This confirms that the mean percentage change of the nominal Mexican interest rate was not different from the United States nominal interest rate.

Levels of the nominal interest rates in Mexico and the United States can differ in equilibrium for many reasons. The small-country assumptions are not inconsistent with this phenomenon. These differences, however, cannot be such that the nominal rate of return (adjusted for transaction costs, risk, and liquidity) on a Mexican instrument is consistently higher or lower than on foreign debt instruments. One can appeal to international arbitrage of debt instruments to insure equilibrium rates of return on Mexican issues vis-a-vis the United States. Though the evidence is not conclusive for Mexico, the author's empirical results do not reject the hypothesis of unified capital markets.

It is even more difficult to make a case for isolated markets in Mexico when, as early as 1963, foreign financing paid for almost 25 percent of public investment. In 1971 Mexico borrowed $1.378 billion from abroad, of which $1.047 billion was borrowed by the government. These figures are remarkable, considering that foreign borrowings were equivalent to 4 percent of GNP. These figures leave little doubt that Mexico is susceptible to the influence of foreign capital markets.

Government policies have been directed at maintaining a rate of interest on Mexican bonds sufficiently high to attract foreign savings; this high rate of interest is due to a liquidity and risk premium paid on Mexican bonds. As noted in Chapter 3, there is no developed secondary bond market in Mexico and, as a result, the actual price of bonds is not determined in a well-functioning market, as is the case in the United States. However, the trend of the Mexican nominal rate of interest has been down relative to the United States rate, despite continuous economic statements that Mexico depends upon its "high" interest rates to attract savings. It is much more likely that the differential rates of interest are due to market conditions determined by costs of holding Mexican bonds vis-a-vis a similar issue in the United States, although interest rate adjustments may lag because of the nature of the bond market.

Since Mexico has displayed an ability to meet its outstanding debt, one would anticipate that differentials would fall. However, the reason for the decreasing risk of a Mexican issue is more involved. The financial sector showed a rapid rate of growth, for most of 1954–74, of between 15 and 16 percent (measured in nominal assets). Maturation of most Mexican financial institutions apparently accelerated during the 1960s and early 1970s. Finally, it is apparent that the investment atmosphere in Mexico changed dramatically between the 1954 devaluation and the early 1970s; a period of stability and growth nurtured a struggling economy into one that by 1973 ranked thirteenth in the free world in the level of GDP. All of these factors made Mexican securities relatively less risky investments.

Of course the mid-1970s present the opposite story on risk. The expansion of public expenditures, the weakening of savings growth, the necessity to borrow abroad, the expansion of domestic credit, and the increase in domestic inflation all contributed to an increase in the risk of devaluation. Thus, as U.S. rates were declining in 1975 and early 1976, their counterparts in Mexico remained high. The gap further widened through fear of economic instability, inflation, and the peso devaluation.

Policies that have assisted in developing the financial markets and physical resources of the financial community have been important in lowering, not raising, the differential paid by Mexican investors for funds on the international markets. In particular, policies of stability helped to lower the interest rate differential by lowering the costs of holding Mexican issues. The Central Bank did not maintain artificially high interest rate differentials to attract foreign savings to Mexico. If the ultimate goals of monetary policy were to maintain "high" rates of interest, that policy has not been successful. However, if the long-term goal for 1954–74 was to make the nominal cost of borrowing relatively less for Mexico vis-a-vis the rest of the world, then the policies were successful. Only in the variable policy of late 1974, 1975, and 1976 do we find that the stability of flow and the cost of borrowing in Mexico were threatened. Throughout most of the period Mexican policy with respect to the interest rate vis-a-vis the United States promoted credit expansion and lowered its cost to the Mexican consumer.

A SUMMARY OF MONETARY, FISCAL, AND DEVELOPMENT POLICIES: 1954-74

We shall briefly examine the Mexican experience since 1954 by analyzing five periods: the devaluation period, 1954-55; the period of growing stability, 1956-60; the period of stability, 1961-68; the transitional period, 1969-71; and the period of economic disruption, 1971 to the present.

Devaluation, 1954-55

The devaluation of 1954 led to a negative trade balance, but it was reversed by 1955. The balance-of-payments position declined in 1954, reflecting the trade deficit and a weak capital account, while in 1955 total reserves increased by $201.5 million. However, in 1955 the trade surplus accounted for only 16.9 percent of the total reserve increase. The remaining portion was a result of the very strong capital account.

Another immediate effect of the devaluation was the dramatic rise in the inflation rate in Mexico. Following a deflation in 1953, the rate rose to above 15 percent in 1955. The monetary approach to the balance-of-payments model indicates that the major contributors to foreign reserve determination in 1955 were decreases in domestic credit, growth in real income, and higher prices. The decrease in domestic credit was a deliberate policy choice of the Central Bank, which rearranged its asset portfolio away from government bonds and loans to foreign reserves.

The price movements, the reserve movements, and the trade balance alterations were results of short-term policies implemented by the Central Bank. First, import substitution became further entrenched and began to dictate fiscal policy actions. Second, new tax laws were instituted in 1955 that later influenced fiscal financing of the government. Finally, the extensive use of the required reserve mechanism as a policy tool in 1954 and 1955 became more influential, resulting in greater dependence of the federal government upon the financing sector. The year 1954 marked the first time that any substantial proportion of government receipts came from borrowing.

Period of Stabilization, 1956-60

During 1956-60 the price level was aligned more closely with that of the United States. The inflation rate decreased, and in 1956 and 1957 reached a level commensurate with that of most industrialized nations. Real income made excellent strides, with the annual rate of growth at about 8 percent. The trade account became negative again, and reserves began to flow outward after the dramatic inflows of 1955. The year 1958 was pivotal for Mexico, as speculation on a devaluation helped create a 16.23 percent decline in foreign reserves. As it became apparent, however, that Mexico was not going to devalue again, the change in reserves was positive in 1959 and has remained so since then. One may conclude from this experience that regardless of the movements in the trade account, the authorities may obtain a positive balance of payments if monetary policy consistent with the monetary approach to the balance is followed.

In 1956–60 the goals of monetary policy were achieved and its rules were maintained. The money supply grew at a rate commensurate with the goals of monetary policy, and the Central Bank used direct loans and discounting to promote sectoral credit allocation. Government deficit financing was achieved without major increases in government securities held by the Central Bank, and the inflation rate was stabilized.

With the increasing ability of the private sector to generate high rates of savings, import substitution became a stronger force. Industrialization in Mexico encountered the typical structural bottlenecks associated with import-substitution policies. Reynolds reports that in 1960, two-thirds of industry was operating below capacity and the prevailing technology "did not appear to be optimal from the point of view of resource allocation."[6]

This period continued to show a rise in the percentage of total government receipts marshaled through borrowing. While 9.78 percent of total receipts was from borrowing in 1956, the figure was about 30 percent of total receipts in 1960.

The growth in the financial sector and the stability of the economy were reflected in movements of the K ratio for the period. K showed a strong downward trend for the period, with only a slight increase in 1958 as a result of reactions to expectations of devaluation. The fall in r during the period can be attributed mainly to a decline in e rather than in required reserves. The money multiplier remained fairly stable, as it did for most of 1956–60, showing only a small increase due to the movements of K and r.

Period of Stability, 1961–68

Monetary and fiscal policies during 1961–68 were also consistent with development policy. Monetary policy was aimed at shifting savings from the private to the public sector. Sectoral allocation via direct loans was promoted until demands of public expenditure caused a shift in policy during the mid-1960s away from private assets to public assets. Growth in domestic credit times foreign reserves over high-powered money increased 7–8 percent annually, and the rate of inflation was very close to that of the United States.

The effect of government borrowing began to stabilize in the 1960s, though a change in the nature of the borrowing occurred. Gradually borrowing (during 1965–68) was decreased in the private and semiprivate sectors as government securities were purchased by the Central Bank. Fiscal expenditures grew at a rate not significantly different from the rate of growth in real income. The ability to tax the new middle class became apparent just as the inability or unwillingness to tax profits occurred (import-substitution policies depended upon high rates of private investments and, therefore, tax progressivity was sacrificed).

During this period international policy was not disrupted because a significant positive capital account made up for a weakening trade balance. Foreign reserve flows in the form of loans or direct investment were actively sought by the financial community and development planners. Though the trade balance was negative, policy makers did not view the fact with trepidation, since the mix in exports was changing from primary and agricultural products to manufactured goods. Import substitution had the side effect of weakening the agricultural sector because it financed industrialization. The government decision was to place greater emphasis on the balance of payments. That is, the balance of trade is only one account that makes up the balance of payments, and is counteracted or reinforced by the capital account in its effect on the balance of payments.

Period of Transition, 1969–71

The period 1969–71 saw a disruption in the orderly policies of the government and the Central Bank. The rate of inflation began to increase worldwide; and the ability of the Central Bank to keep the money supply growing at a rate approximating real income growth was in jeopardy. In 1970, in an attempt to slow the rate of inflation, the Mexican authorities decreased the growth rate in public expenditures. It followed the guidelines of the 1950s and 1960s, and lowered public investment. At the same time there was a decrease in gross domestic product in 1971, as well as a decrease in private sector demand for credit.

The years 1969 and 1970 were transitional for Mexico. With the diluted effectiveness of monetary policy and a greater deficit in trade (the negative balance was $761.5 million), this period witnessed a mixture in economic indicators. After the stable growth in aggregates that prevailed in the mid-1960s, one observed increased inflation in 1970 and 1971. The international difficulties with the dollar exchange were worrisome to the Central Bank. Since the decision was made to continue to peg the peso to the dollar, movements of the dollar were reflected in the peso. The tight monetary policy of 1970 led to reserve inflows as domestic credit was reduced. The policy, however, did not slow the growth in the money supply, which continued to rise along with the inflation rate.

Period of Economic Disruption, 1971-74

In 1973 political and economic pressure led to expansion of government expenditures and to growth in domestic credit. However, the policies of the government, both inflationary (as in 1972 and 1973) and deflationary (as in 1969, 1970, and 1971), did not make the inflation rate significantly different from that of the United States, a result consistent with a fixed exchange rate. Mexico was a price taker in the international marketplace, just as a firm is a price taker in a large competitive industry. Since Mexico adhered to a fixed exchange rate, it had no choice but to accept the rate of inflation dictated by forces in a world market over which it had little influence.

The monetary policies did affect reserve flows, domestic credit, and the money multiplier, as anticipated by the monetary approach to the balance of payments. Decreases in the money multiplier in 1971, 1972, and 1973 are results not only of monetary but also of fiscal policy. Monetary policy was aimed directly at lowering the multiplier through required reserve ratios. However, these are controlled largely by the demands of the government for financing from the private sector. Increased expenditure required increased financing, which, in time, required increased mandatory bank reserves as financial expansion slowed. Indirectly fiscal policy affected the K ratio as the latter began to rise as a result of the instability of the 1970s.

In 1971 the policy of constraint on expenditures and domestic credit creation was continued. In late 1971 and early 1972 government expenditure policies were reversed. Increased public expenditure replaced private investment, which was lagging. The increased expenditures could not be financed from fiscal revenues, and the required reserve mechanism was utilized in an attempt to lower the money multiplier during 1970 and 1971. With the recession, real rates of savings fell and less reserves were available from the financial sector. Money creation then became the method of financing the new expenditures available to the Central Bank. In 1972 Central Bank holdings of government fixed-interest securities doubled, while domestic credit rose more than 100 percent and gD(D/H) grew 37 percent. The money multiplier fell and prices rose. The result, as one would anticipate from the monetary approach to the balance of payments, was a net inflow of foreign reserves. With the 1970 recession, and increased political turmoil, monetary and fiscal policies became less consistent with the development policy within whose framework they were to be administered.

CONCLUSIONS

The Central Bank of Mexico and the Ministry of Finance, which perform functions similar to those of the United States Treasury, were charged with maintenance of a monetary policy commensurate with a fixed exchange rate, sectoral allocation of credit, government deficit financing, infrastructure development financing, regulation of private and semipublic financial institutions, setting legal reserve requirements, acting as banker of the federal government, and managing the money supply. Analysis of the bank and ministry activities since the devaluation of 1954 shows several important conclusions. The Central Bank can encourage, and until recently had done so, a climate such that Mexican risk premiums on debt instruments are lessened. Monetary policy can be used to direct savings from the private to the public sector. Although the Central Bank cannot independently control the money supply of Mexico, it can set domestic credit creation and the money multiplier. Independently, however, the Central Bank cannot control foreign reserve levels, and consequently loses its ability to control the money supply. In association with the private or public sector, it chose the avenues of domestic credit creation through direct loans to the public and private sectors, the private and public banking community, and the federal government.

In conclusion, the monetary and fiscal policies of the 1950s and 1960s were compatible with the maintenance of a fixed exchange rate. During the 1970s, the rules of the monetary policy of the 1960s were more difficult to maintain because development policy burdened the Central Bank's ability to deficit-finance. These policies of the 1970s were sometimes at odds with those suggested by our hypothesis. However, at no time during 1954–74 can one find empirical data results inconsistent with the monetary approach to the balance of payments. The 1954–56 experience with prices and reserves is as expected, given the declines in domestic credit creation and price adjustment.

The long history of stability during the late 1950s and 1960s and the positive balance of payments are consistent with the monetary approach of the balance-of-payments theory, given that growth in domestic credit was at a rate that did not satisfy domestic demand for money. Even during the 1970s, although the decision makers attempted to use monetary policy to slow the rate of the money supply below the rate of growth in money demand, the consequences of monetary policy were consistent with the predictions of the monetary approach to the balance of payments. Only during 1975–76 did we find results, even during the short run, that could be called inconsistent with the monetary approach; however, with the devaluation and a careful study of the policies of all government sectors during 1975 and 1976, one can understand why in the long run the monetary model was consistently a good methodology for understanding the consequences of policy decisions.

NOTES

1. See Dwight S. Brothers and Leopoldo Solis, *Mexican Financial Development* (Austin: University of Texas Press, 1966); Robert L. Bennett, *The Financial Sector and Economic Development* (Baltimore: Johns Hopkins, 1965); Raymond W. Goldsmith, *The Financial Experience of Mexico* (Paris: OECD, 1966); Arturo Ruíz Equihua and Leopoldo Solis, "Aspectos generales de los instrumentos de política monetaria y crediticia en México," unpublished working paper, Centro de Estudios Monetarios Latinamericanos, IX Reunión Operativa, Buenos Aires, November 1968; and Gilberto Escobedo, "Mexican Stabilization Policy, Fiscal or Monetary," working paper, Bank of Mexico, 1973.

2. Mort Gabriel, "El banco central en el fomento de mercados financieros eficaces: Algunas experiencias mexicanas," address to Fourth Meeting of Governors of Central Banks of the Americas, May 1967, p. 1.

3. G. H. Borts and J. A. Hanson, "The Monetary Approach to the Balance of Payments," unpublished working paper, Brown University, 1975.

4. John K. Thompson, "Financial Markets Development as a Technique for Achieving Non-Inflationary Growth: Mexico, 1954-1965," manuscript, Federal Reserve Bank of New York, 1976, p. 10.

5. Clark Reynolds, *The Mexican Economy* (New Haven: Yale University Press, 1970), pp. 286-88; Bennett, op. cit., pp. 115-16; Goldsmith, op. cit., p. 55; Escobedo, op. cit., pp. 5-12.

6. Reynolds, op. cit., p. 189.

6

DIRECTIONS IN MEXICAN
MONETARY POLICIES, 1945-76

In the preceding chapter we summarized the role of the monetary authorities during the critical 1954-74 period. This chapter will reinforce, enlarge upon, and draw from sections of Chapter 5 to trace the historical development of the instruments of, and the actual monetary policies of, the period since the mid-1950s. First, the policy of the period 1945-54 is reviewed. Second, the period of stability and conservative monetary policy, which began with the 1954 devaluation and ended about 1970, is analyzed. Finally, attention is focused on the period of "disruption" (1970-76).* This chapter relates economic development policy, fiscal policy, and social influences to monetary policy. At times we digress to discuss the development of an institution or analyze a particular phenomenon; however, the chapter deals mainly with factors influencing monetary policy during 1954-76. The digressions are allowed only to the extent that they clarify or provide information about the role of monetary policy in Mexican development.

THE FIRST PERIOD: 1945-54

The 1945-54 period was marked by the initiation of import substitution as an economic development policy. World War II provided the stimulus. The industrial countries were engaged in producing war material, rather than consumer

---

*The third period cannot be as clearly separated from the second as can the second from the first. World economic disruptions and changes in domestic policy coincided to mark an end of the earlier period, not with a devaluation, as in 1954, but more gradually, with subtle changes in policy attitudes and goals.

goods. This provided a natural vacuum that Mexican industry could fill without the threat of foreign competition. With the world at war, Mexico experienced both widened demand for its natural resources and increased economic growth. At the end of World War II, Mexico supplemented its historic protection policies with rapid economic development through import substitution combined with the requisite tariff structure. The government began expanded deficit financing for public investment. Fiscal policies led to rapid inflation and instability in the monetary sector, and there were variations in economic growth and instability in the rate of exchange. The devaluation of 1954 ended this period.

The postwar period witnessed policies pursuant to President Miguel Alemán's (1946-52) stated slogan of industrialization. No longer provided with the natural trade protection of World War II, Mexico was faced with a balance-of-payments problem. Commercial policy again was used to stem the reserve losses. Increased production and import substitution, along with devaluation, were the order of the day. As usual, increased protection without the associated restrictive monetary policies did not, in itself, solve the balance-of-payments deficit. Mexico entered a period of devaluation and fiscal investment expansion. Imports helped promote domestic manufacturing, government investment tended to provide the much-needed infrastructure development, and the war helped increase demand for exports; nevertheless, these policies, financed by domestic credit creation, did not correct the worsening balance of payments. Following the devaluation of 1948, inflation hit 10 percent in 1948-49 and 20 percent during 1950, following the 1949 devaluation. Prices leveled out in late 1951 and even fell in 1952-53 as equilibrium in Mexican and world prices was being reestablished. However, the fiscal expansion of 1951 through the first year of President Adolfo Ruíz Cortines (1952-58) was still associated with reserve losses. Mexico was again faced with devaluation in 1954.*

---

*It has been argued, probably justifiably, that the 1954 devaluation was unnecessary to cure the balance-of-payments problem. As we have seen from our analysis, reserve flows are a result of excess demands or supplies of money. During the early 1950s, preceding the devaluation, even with inflation under control, reserves were being lost. Expenditures were financed by passive monetary policy, and that policy was expansionary. Increased government expenditure, financed by the monetary authorities, provided an excess level of money to the public, which used these funds to increase expenditures. A great deal of these funds flowed abroad; for instance, imports in 1951 were 66 percent over the 1950 level. Thus, with inflation growth at world levels, the loss in reserves was more likely a result of excess supplies of money than of disequilibrium in price levels. Perhaps the 1954 devaluation could have been avoided if the monetary policy of the post-1954 devaluation had been adopted a year earlier. However, it can be argued that the devaluation itself was the impetus necessary to bring about the policy that would provide a stable balance of payments.

THE SECOND PERIOD: 1954–70

The second period, 1954–70, began at Easter of 1954, when the peso was devalued from 8.65 to 12.50 per dollar. The exchange rate remained at this level until September 1, 1976, thereby providing an interesting test case for the monetary approach to the balance of payments. The government maintained three goals for monetary policy during this period. The first was to preserve a stable or fixed exchange rate.* The second was to finance government debt, not necessarily through excessive increases in domestic credit but through transfer of funds from financial intermediaries to the government by imposing reserve obligations on *financieras*, savings banks, mortgage banks, and commercial banks. The third was to increase relative growth in those sectors viewed as strategic to maximizing economic growth. To complement fiscal policy, the monetary authorities developed systems of selective credit control, rediscounting, savings, incentives, and savings redistribution. The monetary systems or instruments of policy were tailored to insure that strategic sectors of the economy would have credit available (usually at the expense of other, "less critical" sectors).

The policy of the Mexican government during this period was to maintain the "proper" mix of private and government investment designed to maximize economic growth through import substitution, given the exchange rate constraint. To attract investment, a policy of protective tariffs for infant industries, along with tax incentives for both domestic and foreign investment, was utilized. Though Mexican participation in business investment has been considered essential since the 1917 revolution, foreign investment during this period (and at the present time) was openly sought. Foreign funds in the form of direct investment and savings were actively solicited through a set of investment and tax incentives. Where domestic savings did not fulfill investment demand, government policy provided an atmosphere in which foreign savers could find a return adequate for them to invest in Mexican securities and institutions.

Foreign sources, therefore, provided much of the money necessary to help maintain sustained economic growth. Thus, the exchange rate emerged as an important factor in political, as well as economic, decision making. The government felt that a stable rate of exchange must be maintained if it was to attract the savings (domestic as well as foreign) needed to finance development.

---

*The maintenance of a fixed exchange rate has become a political as well as an economic question. Conversations between the author and officers of the Central Bank in 1975 suggested that the exchange rate, in the view of government officials, had to be maintained if Mexico was to avoid capital flight and currency speculation.

Given that foreign and domestic savings were relied upon to provide the required savings for financing private and public investment, dependence upon the Central Bank for deficit financing was reduced. Thus, the Mexican government planned to nurture development by a set of rules designed to maintain steady growth in public and private investment without excessive inflation, with increased capitalization, and with the maintenance of fixed exchange rates.

The following rules, though not legislated, were generally observed by the government authorities during 1946–70. First, the government would increase its deficit spending only at a rate equal to or just greater than the rate of real economic growth. Second, public investment was to grow at a rate equal to or slightly greater than the rate of real growth. Third, money supply expansion would take place at a rate only slightly greater than real economic growth. These rules provided the framework for economic policy during the 1955–70 period in which monetary policy was used in financing government deficit without excessive money creation. The policies resulted in stable real growth with low levels of inflation, approximating the world rate. Thus, the plan emphasized a dynamic fiscal expenditure policy along with complementary monetary policy. Further, the rules could easily be followed, since the Treasury required low levels of domestic credit creation to service the government debt or to satisfy money demand during the period. Maintenance of the three rules of monetary and fiscal policy, in the opinion of this author, was a most important factor contributing to economic growth without major resource misallocation and periodic economic disruptions, which marked much of Latin American economic activity during the period.

Import Substitution and Policy

In evaluating the importance of these rules in maintaining economic stability, it is useful to begin by establishing the framework for economic development pursued by Mexican planners during the period. Mexico accepted the theory of Raul Prebisch and the Economic Commission of Latin America that development is synonymous with industrialization. Once it had experienced the growth in industrial production fostered by World War II, and had accepted the Prebisch hypothesis of deterioration of terms of trade for raw materials producers,[1] industrialization was the logical development choice. The process of industrialization through import substitution makes capital relatively less expensive than labor. The policy recognizes the misallocation associated therewith, but accepts it as a necessary evil.

Import-substitution policies demand a tariff structure that promotes capital goods importation, while discouraging that of consumer goods. It also leads to dependence upon foreign sources for increased capital formation, theoretically up to the point where the economy can support "efficient" industries that can compete in the world market. This type of policy also calls for a redistribution of resources from the agricultural and primary goods sectors to the industrial sector. Usually tax and tariff incentives accompany the industrialization. To attract investment, the government must insure returns above what would be normal in a fully competitive economy. The government may provide these incentives by creating monopolies, by creating a tax structure favorable to the industrial sector, by openly redirecting investment to the sector, or by directly subsidizing the sector. Alternatively, monetary policy can be used to direct savings into various sectors through credit rationing procedures at "low" interest rates. To a certain extent Mexico has undertaken a mixture of all these policy alternatives.

The fiscal policies that complement industrialization—particularly tax incentives, subsidies, and discriminatory tariff structures—lead to an unresponsive revenue generating mechanism; that is, the overall revenue-income elasticity coefficient for government is low. The incentives for private investment gear the tax structure to ensure high levels of private investment; however, by its very nature, the tax structure does not generate required resources for increased public investment and expanded social services. As the protected sector increases in relative importance, revenue generation through the tax base cannot increase relative to expenditures if the percentages of private and public investment are to be maintained.

In the period following the devaluation, therefore, the burden of government financing could not be maintained by revenues from fiscal resources (the national lottery, income tax, corporation taxes, tariffs, fees). While one may ask why these revenue sources could not be enlarged to increase public investment, it is clear that the nature of Mexican development policies required low tax rates on investment, tax incentives on new industrial investment, subsidies via monopoly, credit guarantees, tax incentives on income earned from savings, and fiscal incentives for foreign investment (guarantees, patents, and so on). Such policies must be maintained to ensure industrial sector growth; however, as this sector grows relative to the others, new tax legislation has not provided a revenue offset to industrial tax exemption. Federal interference with these tax exemptions would be counterproductive to stimulating private investment, both foreign and domestic.

The Mexican government was therefore plagued with deficits if the ratio of private to public expenditures was to be maintained. The deficits could be financed by several policies, including foreign borrowing, domestic bond sales, diversion of savings from the private to the public sector through the commercial banking sector, and printing money. Many of the less developed countries during this period financed government deficits through creation of new money. Since excessive monetary expansion led to massive deficits in the balance of payments, with accompanying capital outflow, inflation-plagued nations utilized exchange rate controls, and finally devaluation, in order to pursue independent monetary policy. Mexico chose to utilize all methods of debt financing available to it, placing relatively less dependence upon domestic credit creation. The development path implemented by Mexican planners thus required that government expenditures be partially financed through the monetary sector. Therefore, Mexican monetary policy necessarily has been largely determined by and responsible to economic development policies.

Tools of Monetary Policy

As indicated earlier, the government had available a series of monetary tools, including foreign borrowing, domestic land sales, reserve requirements, obligatory reserve government bonds, domestic credit creation, sectoral allocation, individual bank stimulation, and rediscounting. All were utilized during 1954-70 under the set of specific rules. One of the most important functions of monetary policy was to finance the government deficit without increasing money supply more rapidly than money demand. The policy of the Central Bank and the government was to utilize monetary policy under the condition that the money supply did not grow at a pace much greater than the rate of growth in real income. The question then arose of how to finance the government debt without risking capital flight and resulting pressures on the balance of payments. In short, the conflict emerged as a result of the twin objectives of maintaining a gradual growth in the money supply while borrowing to finance government deficits. The path selected included mandatory reserve requirements on new deposits that would be partially in the form of government bonds, small increases in domestic credit if needed, and foreign borrowing.

Monetary policy was charged not only with the financing of the government deficit, under constraints, but also with the assistance of development financing through regulating credit in such a way as to stimulate growth. Arturo Ruíz Equihua and Leopoldo Solis summarize this period as follows:

> The economy of Mexico, like the rest of the developing countries, suffers from a relative scarcity of capital. Therefore, the monetary policy has among its basic responsibilities to stimulate the formation of internal savings and its capture on the part of the financial institutions and influence the sectoral allocation of it, with the goal of raising the efficiency of its [savings] use.[2]

They also comment that the instruments utilized to achieve these goals are constrained by the necessity to maintain internal and external economic stability while simultaneously encouraging the confidence of the general public in the banking system as a whole.

The Deficit Problem

Responsibility for financing the government deficit in 1954-70 fell primarily upon the financial sector. The Central Bank provided the funds for public investment that could not be generated by fiscal revenues. The bank was also required to maintain internal and external funds adequate to provide liquidity in the private sector, while transferring some savings directly into the government sector. Mexico did not have a well-developed bond market, and thus the Treasury could not directly solicit large amounts of savings from the domestic private sector through the issuance of government bonds on the scale needed to finance the deficits. In addition, the Central Bank was not allowed to expand the monetary base by significant amounts through domestic credit creation. The compromise program that emerged eventually made government financing dependent upon the private banking community for the funds. Tó insure that the banking system had adequate funds available to allow a shift from the private to the government sector without significantly lowering liquidity to the private sector, monetary policy was designed to increase both internal and external savings.

To facilitate the generation of internal and external savings, "high" rates of interest were maintained. The "high" rates clearly could not be different in nominal terms from the world rate because of arbitrage in world bond markets. To maintain a rate of interest that would prevent capital flight, the Mexican banking system paid a liquidity premium, enabling an equilibrium rate to be maintained that was greater, in absolute terms, than that in the United States.* Incentives such as decreased taxes on income derived from savings were introduced. Semigovernmental and governmental savings institutions (*financieras*) grew in importance. The general financial structure increased in physical size as well as in assets over this period of stability.

Monetary authorities stressed the importance of the development of these institutions for the filtering of the necessary funds into the financial mainstream. It was felt that the financial structure of the economy needed development because, without it, many segments of society would be outside the financial community, with the possible result of a loss in their savings resources. Ruíz Equihua and Solis comment, ". . . one of the principal objectives of the monetary policy of the Bank of Mexico and the financial authorities resides in stimulation of equilibrium growth of the financial system, with the basic goal

---

*Some Mexican authors have noted that the "high" rates of interest are simply equilibrium rates that are greater in absolute terms to cover exchange risk and transactions costs. See Gilberto Escobedo, "Ahorra y desarrollo económico," Bank of Mexico working paper, 1975, p. 18.

of capturing a volume of the growth in savings of the public. . . ."[3] Along with the "high" rate of interest, economic stability, and other monetary stimulants for raising the level of savings within the financial system, fiscal incentives were offered as a device to increase the nominal amount of interest paid on savings.

Assuming the availability of funds within the financial community to satisfy the public debt, the Central Bank and the monetary authorities created a system of reserve requirements that would transfer funds from the private and semiprivate institutions by a program wherein a percentage of the reserves held against deposits could be in the form of government bonds. These bonds were low-interest-bearing and could be used to replace deposits as reserves at the Central Bank.

Bonds could be utilized for a percentage of the reserves on hand at the bank, the figure to vary according to the type and date of deposit, type and location of the institution, and whether the deposit was in pesos or another currency.* In essence, these bonds acted as a transfer of money from the private to the public sector. The transfer could be regulated by a committee of the Central Bank, utilizing the required reserve ratios. This is the Mexican version of the Open Market Committee of the U.S. Federal Reserve System.

There are several important points related to this type of financing. First, since deficit spending depends upon transfers of funds from the private to the public sector through the banking system, the government becomes dependent upon the private and semigovernmental banking system for funds. Second, if any policy of the government disturbs the amount of savings captured by the domestic banking system, the ability of the system to feed the investment portfolio of the government is lessened. For example, any governmental actions that cause a decrease in real savings will lower the amount of funds available for public investment. Third, if the rate of growth of the deficit is greater than the savings rate, the availability of private investment liquidity is lowered. Fourth, perhaps the most important point to note is that this reserve mechanism does not carry the traditional multiplier effect that a Central Bank required-

---

*Reserve requirements in Mexico are very complicated. While all financial institutions must maintain required reserves with the Central Bank, only deposit banks have the ability to create money. There are two types of reserves. One is the traditional noninterest-bearing deposits by the banks at the Banco de México, while the second can be held in the form of low-interest-bearing government securities. The latter reserve requirement is clearly a transfer of funds from the private to the public sector.

The second form of reserve requirement is a tool that may be utilized to transfer from the private to the public sector, but it may not be used to control the money supply. It is extremely difficult to separate exactly what the average reserve requirement is for Mexico, since the reserve structure is composed of these two types of reserves and requirements on individual banks vary with location and classification within a bank category, as well as across categories.

reserve held deposit would.* The reserve requirement in the form of government bonds has been a part of the Mexican financial structure since 1947, when reserve requirements were placed on demand deposits. They were extended to the savings departments in 1955. Finally, in 1957 reserve requirements were imposed on the *financieras*. Direction and control of these obligatory deposits were given to the Central Bank, to be utilized as a Mexican version of the open market operation.

While the open market operation in the United States can clearly direct the movements in the money supply, it is suggested that such is not necessarily the case with the adjustment of marginal reserves held in the form of government bonds. Studies by members of the Central Bank of Mexico have indicated that the use of these reserve requirements to control the money supply has had little effect. The question, however, is whether these reserve requirements have affected the multiplier, not the supply of money. In 1971 there was an attempt to lower the rate of increase in the money supply. Though it had little effect on the stock of money, a sharp decline in the money multiplier was recorded.

The result of such financing is clear, in that its impact upon liquidity for private investment will be lessened as the banks transfer funds from the private to the public sector. This transference mechanism is needed, however, because the process of economic development, as seen by the Mexican authorities during this period, demanded large amounts of investment in infrastructure to provide the balanced and stable growth necessary to maintain internal and external stability. A movement away from this equilibrium path would result in a strain on one sector or the other, with spillover effects to all sectors. Clearly, a dramatic rise in government spending that would call for an amount greater than available savings would entail a decrease in private liquidity and investment. Alternatively, if domestic credit were increased to provide the depleted private liquidity, pressures would be placed on the balance of payments and produce undesirable effects on the financial structure. Any disruption in the financial structure implies a loss in captured savings for Mexico. Thus, the movement by one sector from equilibrium causes a cumulative cycle. The difficulty lies in the nature of the financial structure in Mexico, which is constrained by its development plan and required fiscal and monetary policy.

One can see the importance of the rules that were adopted by the governmental authorities during the period of stability. With these rules, the monetary

---

*The multiplier effect of an increase in the traditional reserve requirement is to lower the multiplier, and therefore to lower the money supply. In the early 1970s Mexico increased marginal reserve requirements in an effort to slow the growth in the supply of money. These policies had little effect on the money supply. The effect is to shift financial resources from the private sector to the public sector—that is, a forced loan to the government in the form of bonds.

authorities were able to maintain the stability in the financial community upon which the development program depended. During this period of low inflation worldwide, a monetary expansion policy such as dictated by the three rules was most appropriate.

Growth of the Financial Sector

The expansion and dynamization of the financial sector has been a policy objective for the Mexican government during all three periods. As indicated in Table 6.1, financial sector growth occurred primarily during the 1954–70 period of stability. Since the development process in Mexico was tied closely to the amount of savings that could be generated, it was important that the financial sector grow physically so that it could capture increased savings. A greater geographic spread of savings and commercial banks was required, as was a general increase in the number and diversity of financial institutions. The Nacional Financiera emerged as an important instrument in providing a safe outlet for

TABLE 6.1

Number of Mexican Credit Institutions, 1950–70
(as of December 31)

Type of Institution	1950	1954	1958	1962	1966	1970
Official	24	27	41	40	194	295
Banco de México	8	9	11	11	19	13
Others	16	18	30	29	175[a]	282
Private	570	677	1,102	1,300	1,649	2,023
Deposit	414	526	898	1,091	1,434	1,814
Investment	99	97	120	132	132	131
Others	57	54	84	77	83	78
Banking departments	406	516	1,479	1,739	2,484	3,228
Savings	313	416	886	1,005	1,462	1,840
Trust	93	100	593	634	922	1,388
Auxiliary credit institutions[b]	100	120	118	117	126	131

Note: Figures include branch offices.

[a]The large increase in the number of official institutions is a result of increasing branch offices.

[b]Includes warehouses, credit unions, clearinghouses, and securities exchanges.

Source: Statistics on the Mexican Economy (Mexico City: Nacional Financiera, 1974), pp. 215–21.

TABLE 6.2

Assets of the Mexican Banking System, 1954-73
(million pesos, as of December 31)

	Private Institutions		Official Institutions		
	Deposit and Savings	Others	Bank of Mexico	Nacional Financiera	Other Official
1954	8,114.8	2,438.4	7,949.3	3,015.6	7,909.0
1955	10,020.2	2,927.5	9,009.4	2,498.2	5,709.8
1956	11,082.0	3,808.8	9,935.0	2,435.2	6,700.1
1957	12,367.5	4,874.9	10,428.8	2,944.2	6,885.2
1958	13,492.5	6,091.4	11,328.7	3,642.8	7,919.7
1959	15,049.4	8,126.7	12,421.2	4,139.4	9,246.1
1960	16,253.7	10,462.9	13,204.6	7,751.1	10,622.5
1961	17,648.6	12,687.3	14,587.7	10,047.4	11,464.3
1962	19,880.0	15,374.4	16,074.4	12,051.3	12,296.1
1963	23,214.4	19,968.6	18,373.3	13,761.7	14,300.8
1964	27,808.6	26,086.7	19,928.3	14,611.5	17,678.8
1965	30,458.4	31,140.5	20,723.0	16,149.7	20,920.4
1966	34,072.8	40,347.7	23,329.9	19,248.9	23,655.8
1967	37,098.2	49,108.7	25,707.3	23,830.3	26,633.2
1968	42,750.2	58,525.8	29,844.7	27,704.9	29,191.3
1969	49,261.7	73,562.5	33,206.7	30,989.9	32,807.7
1970	54,027.7	90,927.3	36,353.2	34,028.8	35,860.4
1971	59,434.6	107,690.4	41,494.8	36,601.6	47,394.6
1972	67,667.8	124,982.0	67,238.8	41,400.2	53,333.6
1973	84,408.0	135,119.9	89,696.5		117,869.1*

*Includes Nacional Financiera.

Source: Statistics of the Mexican Economy (Mexico City: Nacional Financiera, 1974), pp. 255-59.

domestic savings. Further, the Nacional Financiera has played a major role in financing infrastructure development through direct loans to the public sector, as well as through the reserve transference mechanism. Other types of financial institutions have grown dramatically. Mort Gabriel, in a presentation to the Fourth Meeting of Governors of the Central Banks of the Americas, noted: ". . . the resources of the banking system have increased at an annual rate of 16.4 percent, having passed from 5,000 million pesos in 1946 to 105,000 million pesos in 1966."[4]

The rapid increase in financial resources, as noted by Gabriel, is a critical input into the Mexican development if balanced and consistent policies are to be maintained (see Table 6.2). The role of the monetary authorities in objectively enlarging the size of the financial sector cannot be minimized. The stabilizing monetary policies of 1954-70 helped to move the currency-to-deposit ratio from greater than 1 in 1954 to approximately 0.7 in 1970, which indicates the increased utilization of the banking system by the public. The Central Bank helped foster the expansion of the financial community by providing services such as rediscounting. Again, the active role of the Central Bank in the daily operation of the financial community gave impetus to the stability of individual banks. Government regulations on the role of commercial banks vis-a-vis *financieras*, both public and private, was a move toward stabilization of the sector. In essence, the most important policy factor for the growth of the financial community lay in the economic stability of the period coupled with monetary policy that helped to insure financial stability.

Private and public *financieras* increased their relative importance in the Mexican financial structure during this period, gaining dominance over the commercial banking system in terms of total assets. Designed to capture savings that perhaps would not otherwise enter the financial sector, the *financieras* experienced a growth in relative participation in the capital markets much greater than the overall growth rate of the sector. During the early 1950s, regulations were enacted that stimulated returns on liabilities offered by private *financieras*. The Central Bank actively sought to liberalize regulations concerning allocation of loanable funds to the *financieras* and to change the yield from their deposits in order to promote wealth-portfolio adjustments in their favor. In 1954 the annual growth rate in assets of private *financieras* was approximately 25 percent, in 1959 approximately 40 percent, and in 1966 about 30 percent. Though these rates of change are comparatively large, in no year between 1954 and 1970 did the annual growth rate become negative. In most cases the annual figure was around 20 percent.[5]

Raymond Goldsmith comments of this period:

> *Nacional Financiera* represents probably the most important original contribution by Mexico to the types of financial institutions participating in financing economic development and promoting economic growth. . . . *Nacional Financiera* is characterized by its pragmatic character and its combination of features of public and private enterprise.[6]

Nacional Financiera has continued to grow steadily since its inception in 1934. During 1954-70, it rapidly expanded its resources through foreign borrowing as well as by capturing domestic savings. Its share of assets of the total financial system rose to about 12 percent during the late 1950s and remained steady throughout the period. The government desired to make funds available for infrastructure development. More than half of the Nacional Financiera's loans during the period were for infrastructure projects. It is apparent that this semigovernmental agency is important not only in capturing savings but also in redirecting funds into public works.

The discount mechanism can be used to regulate the rate of growth in deposits of individual banks. The Central Bank may use the discount window at will to stimulate deposits in given commercial banks. During 1954-70 it maintained a target rate of growth in deposits for various commercial banks. Whether or not a bank was expanding its deposits at this rate was important in the Central Bank's decision to make funds available. Naturally the discount mechanism had other uses that infringed upon its use solely for controlling the expansion of deposits; but, where possible, it was frequently utilized to maintain steady growth in the financial sector as a whole and among individual banks.

In summary, the government has, through the Central Bank, the Ministry of Finance and Public Credit, and the Nacional Financiera, made a concerted effort to expand financial services in Mexico. Though the demand for these services existed and probably would have evolved, the concerted effort of government policy to establish an advanced banking system cannot be overestimated. The structure of the financial system and the spectrum of services provided clearly complemented the Mexican economic development plan during this period.

Sectoral Credit Allocation

The allocation of credit to particular sectors of the economy is viewed by the Mexican Central Bank as one of its most important functions. Ernesto Fernández Hurtado, director general of the Bank of Mexico, alluded to geographic and sectoral allocation in the opening remarks of a convention address at Jalisco:

> The Bank of Mexico directed regional development through the application of its instruments of credit regulation. . . . Moreover, by the means of selective channeling of credit and the redistribution of resources that affect the funds for stimulating agricultural, industrial, and living standards activities, it has applied a dedicated and vigorous policy of redirecting [reinvesting] and channeling credit resources to the province. . . .[7]

These remarks are enlightening as to the importance assigned by the Central Bank to sectoral credit allocation as an instrument of monetary policy. Direct channeling, differential reserve requirements, and the discount rate are enumerated as possible tools.

Arturo Ruíz Equihua and Leopoldo Solis comment upon sectoral credit allocation as follows:

> . . . the authorities have utilized from time to time the obligatory deposit mechanism with selectivity.

> In the first place, the commercial banks ought to channel no less than 70 percent of . . . active operation into financing production and no more than 30 percent to commerce; the same orientation should be observed in relative norms with respect to obligatory deposits of finance companies, although no proportion is expressly established.[8]

They suggest that sectoral reallocation from commerce to production is a necessary part of the development scheme. For example:

> Furthermore, the financial authorities have marked certain diverse economic sectors with high priority for preferential channeling of the banking resources: industry, agricultural and cattle production, residential and public construction, exportation of manufactured products and the acquisition of consumer durables.[9]

The comments of these three men are important, since they represent the mainstream of Mexican economic thought with respect to sectoral credit allocation.

During 1954–70, the Central Bank attempted, using various means, to allocate credit by sector. One method was simply to direct the financial intermediaries to appropriate certain percentages of their portfolios to particular sectors or industrial endeavors. A second tool was to use the discount window discriminatively with respect both to a bank's loan portfolio and to the particular paper being discounted. A special discount window was in operation to regulate and promote sectoral allocation. A third sectoral credit tool was to differentiate with respect to obligatory reserve requirements among institutions by location, size, and types of lending.

Direct Allocation

The method of direct allocation of funds to strategic sectors, with particular emphasis upon industrial production, was theoretically simple. The Central Bank instructed the individual financial intermediary to direct specified percentages of its resources to industry, agriculture, commerce, external financing, and other sectors. The beauty of this approach is that the financial institution must give the Central Bank information about dispersion in its wealth portfolio; and the Ministerio de Hacienda y Crédito Público, with the Central Bank, utilizes the information to plan the levels of funds directed to strategic sectors. Unfortunately, the disadvantage of this system of credit allocation is that it does not appear to work in practice. Though a tool that is venerated in many speeches and memos of the Central Bank and a policy discussed in the literature,[10] it has met with little success. Indeed, one should take caution in assuming that the allocation policy statements of the Ministry of Finance and the Central Bank can be fully implemented.

The degree to which credit may be allocated directly depends largely on whether or not the "rules" of the Central Bank can be enforced. The financial intermediary's credit portfolio under control of the Central Bank may easily show an allocation of credit consistent with the dictates of the bank, while in fact loans are structured so that allocation is left to the market. For example, financial institutions may be directed by the Central Bank to allocate credit as follows: 40 percent industry, 20 percent large farmer, 20 percent commerce, 10 percent small farmer, 10 percent miscellaneous. The commercial bank can easily loan money to a large farmer to purchase an airplane for crop dusting. Such a plane may be funded out of any of four areas of allocation. The craft itself is a commercial tool. Since a large farmer receives the loan, it may be funded from the "large farmer" allocation. If the large farmer explained that there would be dusting material settling on the small farmer's property, the money could easily be allocated from the small farmer's portfolio allocation. Indeed, the financial intermediary is able to loan at his discretion, as if no controls existed.

Though trite, this example illustrates the difference between theoretical policy and actual credit allocation. It has been the experience of the authorities at the Bank of Mexico that the only effective credit allocation programs are those that lend themselves to Central Bank control, such as discounting.

The Discount Window

An alternative method of credit allocation that became popular with the Central Bank was the use of the discount window. A fund was created for controlling financial allocation through the discount window, and ultimately through the financial intermediaries themselves. The fund is used to discount notes on specific loans made by the commercial banks. Thus the financial institutions must provide full information concerning loan use when the loan is discounted at the Central Bank. The latter is therefore in control of the direction of specific funds. This method has been highly successful in Mexico.

Under the old system, an individual could go to a commercial bank and apply for a loan to purchase a car. If the commercial bank had filled its consumer loan quota, the individual would ask for a loan to build a house. Since this fund would be open, he would receive the loan and proceed to purchase his new automobile. To avoid this behavior the commercial bank—using the discount window—must provide the Central Bank with full information regarding any loan to be discounted. (Essentially, the government compensated the financial intermediaries through the discount mechanism for the extra costs of having a wealth portfolio, which is different from a profit-maximizing portfolio.) The experience of the Mexican Central Bank was, therefore, that enforcement of direct sectoral allocation was more difficult and costly than sectoral allocation through the discount window.

One of the major sources of funds for the sectorally oriented national financial institutions was the Central Bank discount window. By increasing discounting during 1957-74, the Central Bank was able to leverage its control over the portfolio of much of the financial sector. A considerable amount of the discounted paper was in support of various public or quasi-public enterprises. For example, commercial paper of a government agency was often purchased at a low rate of interest and the paper then sold to various financial institutions at attractive yields. Thus, as Dwight Brothers and Leopoldo Solis note, "Rediscounting was combined with a form of open market sales. . . ."[11]

Reserve Requirements

The third method of allocation was to attempt to utilize the obligatory reserve tool as a means of directing credit. Reserve requirements were used to alter the level of deposits for differing classes of intermediaries, depending upon the structure of loan portfolio, physical size, and location. Given a level of reserves that must be held by the financial community to finance the government, differential reserve requirements could be imposed upon commercial banks by geographic location. For example, during a period of agricultural crisis, such as occurred in 1957 and 1958, the Central Bank could redirect some of the government financing burden from the rural banks to the city banks, in order to free resources for agriculture.

In Mexico infrastructure development is financed largely through the *financieras*. A reduction in obligatory reserve requirements for the *financieras* allows relatively more funds to be available for infrastructure investment. Financial institutions fall into different categories, by size and deposits, and are subject to the Central Bank's use of the discount mechanism as well as the obligatory reserve requirement. The obligatory reserve tool can be used individually to provide credit to selected institutions serving strategic sectors.

Concluding Remarks: 1954-70

During 1954-70 Mexico's development plan was consistent, well developed, and substantially important in achieving economic growth. At the same time, it was relatively free from many of the monetary problems plaguing most of the Latin American economy. Government planners implemented their development plan with tenacity. The roles of monetary and fiscal policy were clearly complementary, since fiscal policy was entirely consistent with the selected development path. Monetary policy was passive with respect to development policy and complemented fiscal policy.

Whether one agrees or disagrees with the Prebisch doctrine that import substitution is the appropriate policy for economic development is not an issue for this analysis. Given that Mexico implemented the import-substitution path, one may conclude that the set of rules governing fiscal and monetary policy was consistent with the goals of import-substitution development. The fact that the fiscal policies for federal revenues were relatively income-inelastic with respect to GDP is not a failure on the part of government policy; rather, it is indicative of the overall success of development policies. Given inadequate revenue levels, a policy for capturing and utilizing private resources had to be formulated. The resulting monetary policy responded with noninflationary federal financing through expansion of the financial intermediaries. In short, monetary and fiscal policies were closely coordinated during this period and were fitted to the development path. The response of monetary policy to the economic development plan facilitating the building of institutions was entirely consistent with the domestic economy. Finally, the use of sectoral allocation, although its success was questionable, was also congruous with overall policy objectives.

In summary, the Mexican government adopted a plan of development and coordinated its policies and tools in order to generate a rational plan of development that, when implemented under a set of rules, kept monetary and fiscal policies completely consistent with the original development goal. The most important feature of this period of development is the strict adherence to general guidelines. As long as the stated goals of development were met with consistent policy, and as long as policies could be generated that would carry out these long-run goals, the process was sustainable. However, any breakdown of the rules or disruption of the plan itself would have endangered the entire system. The complementary nature of the policies and the development process generated a viable system. Such was not the case for the period since 1970.

THE THIRD PERIOD: 1970-76

It is difficult to define the beginning of this most recent period, since the period of stability did not come to an abrupt halt in 1970. Indeed, many of the changes in the economy that would mark the end of the second period began in the stable 1950s. The same policies that contributed to stability during the 1950s and 1960s began to disintegrate in the 1970s. The forms of monetary and fiscal policy that were utilized successfully during the period of stability required world economic stability in order to be effective. The 1970s saw disequilibrium in the world economy, worldwide inflation, and world recession; these outside shocks were extremely disruptive to the Mexican economy. A number of the policy goals of the federal government were simultaneously altered. Income redistribution acquired increasing policy importance, and Mexico began to face a crisis in the agricultural sector. The latter had, for many years, been the sector from which the capital necessary to expand industry had flowed. New government attitudes on financing some of the programs emerged. The earlier policies of not expanding the money supply more rapidly than GNP were frequently broken, even though the Central Bank attempted to maintain the standard. The principle requiring that government sale of securities to cover deficits increase at a rate less than, or slightly greater than, the rate of growth in real income was no longer obeyed. All of these changes sent shocks throughout the Mexican monetary sector.

The 1954–70 period of stability bequeathed a development structure to the 1970s that was dependent upon balanced growth in major economic sectors, increased government investment in infrastructure, small government deficits, and increased savings. The third period has seen large government deficits, inflation, increased domestic credit creation, and massive amounts of foreign borrowing in the public sector. The financial sector since 1971 has witnessed a decline in real savings growth. The real growth rate has been erratic. Mexico has turned from an exporter of agricultural products to an importer. Capital flight has increased and foreign investment has slowed. In many ways the "Mexican Miracle" has been much less miraculous during the 1970s.

With the development of the financial sector's role in financing fiscal deficits during the period of stability, the federal government has become increasingly dependent upon the financial community. The fiscal policies needed to reverse the trend in modes of financing public expenditure appear to be outside the import-substitution approach to development. Fiscal resource financing of new government expenditures becomes more difficult, given the import-substitution development process. Therefore, pressure has been placed upon the financial community to support public investment.

The government has maintained that a stable exchange rate between Mexico and the United States is necessary, although the balance of trade is becoming even more negative. A stable exchange rate is so important to the government that increased foreign borrowing is used to bolster the balance of payments.

The Balance of Payments

Tables 6.3 and 6.4 indicate how the deficit in the balance of payments was financed between 1969 and 1973, and they show that government and private borrowing were the major contributors to the overall increase in the capital account. It is also clear that 1973 saw the highest increase, more than doubling the long-term capital account from 1972 to 1973. It should also be noted that public sector borrowing was up by 260 percent in 1973 over 1972 and that private borrowing jumped from $186.3 to $331.3 million. Over the five-year period, nominal direct foreign investment varied little and real direct investment

TABLE 6.3

Trade and Capital Account: Mexico, 1969-73
(million dollars)

Item	1969	1970	1971	1972	1973
Balance of merchandise and services	−472.7	−945.9	−726.4	−761.5	−1,223.4
Net errors and omissions on current account and in capital movements	−172.3	498.7	217.7	233.5	−338.9
Long-term capital	692.9	503.9	669.1	753.5	1,684.6
Special drawing rights	−	45.4	39.6	39.2	−
Change in revenue at Banco de México	47.9	102.1	200.0	264.7	122.3

Sources: Statistics on the Mexican Economy (Mexico City: Nacional Financiera, 1974), pp. 370-72; *International Financial Statistics* (Washington, D.C.: International Monetary Fund); *Indicadores economicas* (Mexico City: Bank of Mexico).

decreased. Though the period exhibits an increased trade deficit, the capital accounts were more than compensating and every year witnessed an increase in foreign reserves, which is consistent with the monetary approach to the balance of payments.

Monetary Policy Flexibility

The data in Tables 6.3 and 6.4 indicate the necessity for the government to seek foreign funds to maintain the exchange rate and finance the debt over the early 1970s. The increased foreign borrowing added dramatically to the stock of high-powered money, but allowed the Central Bank to avoid greater increases in domestic credit to fund government deficits. However, this policy curbed the Central Bank's flexibility in monetary policy. Gilberto Escobedo says:

The necessity for external borrowing to finance the current account deficit of the balance of payments without losing reserves gradually imposed restrictions to the control of the money supply; since this debt only increased again the medium of exchange in the hands of

TABLE 6.4

Loans from Abroad to Mexico, 1969-73
(million dollars)

Item	1969	1970	1971	1972	1973
Loans (net)	468.0	324.4	450.6	546.0	1,377.9
Public sector (net)	–	263.1	286.4	359.7	1,046.6
Private sector	–	61.1	164.2	186.3	331.3
Government debt	–18.8	–2.3	–28.9	37.8	69.9

Sources: Statistics on the Mexican Economy (Mexico City: Nacional Financiera, 1974), pp. 370–72; *International Financial Statistics* (Washington, D.C.: International Monetary Fund); *Indicadores economicas* (Mexico City: Bank of Mexico).

the community, thus increasing its aggregate demand, and very possibly, new demand for new imports. To stop this from happening, the Bank of Mexico would have to compensate in its monetary base for the Nation's expanded supply that the new dollars stimulated.

This compensatory contraction could only be made by limiting its credit, either to private banks or to the government, or by increasing the legal adjustments requisite and sterilizing them (new dollars). In other words, not injecting again these financial resources in the form of credit to the economic system.[12]

Escobedo raises the point that domestic credit must be controlled or high-powered money will increase, thus implying an increase in the money supply. He notes that the increases in the money supply must adjust. The adjustment process, according to Escobedo, would take the form of increased aggregate demand for goods and services provided by the world market. Since the government is concerned with the weakening trade balance, the increased foreign borrowing results in continuous portfolio adjustments, including the trade account. Under the monetary approach to the balance of payments, the period change in monetary aggregate was as anticipated. Though the Central Bank attempted to slow growth in the money supply by decreasing domestic credit growth and the multiplier, the money supply continued to grow as an adjustment was made through the amount of reserves. Indeed, in desiring adherence to the third rule, the Central Bank helped to facilitate large flows of foreign reserves.

However, if increased foreign borrowing, ceteris paribus, leads to future increases in the current account deficit, this policy is contrary to the development goals of import substitution. The difficulty arises as to how government expenditures are financed. Borrowing abroad by the authorities decreases pressure on domestic credit creation, which in turn promotes private market demand for money, thus engendering a balance of payments equilibrium. Since foreign borrowing has been needed to maintain a fixed exchange rate, the logical tools for the Central Bank to use are a lower domestic credit and a decreased multiplier. These options, however, are not independent of development policy. Escobedo observes:

> As the public sector financial requirements were increasing, mainly because of its incapacity to increase tax revenues at the same rate as public expenditures, and as the balance of payments was increasing, the Bank of Mexico has had to tolerate greater increases in the national money supply. . . .[13]

He further notes that these limitations on the monetary policy, when coupled with the deterioration of the rate of savings captured by the banking community in both real and nominal terms, should be grounds for a reevaluation of present development policy.[14] It is clear that the present inflexibility in the tax structure, with its effect on the monetary sector, is a direct result of the import-substitution development plan.

The Central Bank, in responding to increased government demands for financing, raised marginal reserve requirements for obligatory government notes. The net effect on the money supply was relatively small, since these requirements were met with new issues of government bonds. The bonds constituted a transfer, through the banking system, from the private sector; and the effect of the new marginal reserve rates was a decrease in the proportion of funds available to the private sector. There is no information available to indicate that the increased reserve requirements, where the reserves were held in new issues of government debt, had any sizable effect on the money supply. Indeed, as would be expected under the monetary approach to the balance of payments, the money supply continued to grow rapidly.

Economic Policy and the Development Scheme

Since 1970 the Mexican economic development plan has begun to show strain. The path during the 1950s and 1960s eventually made government financing a responsibility of the financial community. In 1969 it became obvious that the public deficit was increasing as the development plan created a diminishing (in relative terms) tax base. Taxes could not generate the revenue necessary to pay for public development expenditures, and government relied upon increasing the debt held by the Central Bank, the private banking community, and the foreign private and public entities.

Recognizing the dilemma in 1970, the government decreased the growth rate in public expenditures. In doing so it attempted to follow the guidelines of the 1950s and 1960s. Coincidental with decreased government investment was a decline in the growth rate of real domestic product in 1971, coupled with a decrease in the demand for credit in the private sector. These 1970 and 1971 restrictive monetary and fiscal policies became untenable for the authorities because growth was being slowed much more rapidly than anticipated. Under the scheme of development during the 1950s and 1960s, however, these tight policies had to be maintained if a stable growth in all sectors was to be achieved.

In 1972 some of the priorities changed. Agricultural development became more important as Mexico was faced with a deteriorating manufacturing sector. Government began to place a greater priority on income redistribution while still espousing the scheme of import-substitution development, with its demands upon the economy. For the first time since 1954, government policy began to conflict with the overall development goals.

The 1972 goals were in contrast with the policy of 1970-71, and a new monetary and fiscal policy was adopted. In order to increase total government expenditure, controls were loosened in 1972, and real domestic product and consumption began to accelerate. Since 1971 government debt has increased at an annual rate of 50 percent and government foreign borrowing has increased even more rapidly. External debt has increased almost threefold, and the balance-of-trade deficit has increased from $761.5 million in 1972 to approximately $2,500 million in 1974.

Further distortions in the development scheme are evident with the decrease in the rate of demand for savings by the private sector. The decline could possibly be attributed to the private sector's loss of confidence in the economic stability of Mexico as the conflict between policy and development objectives became more apparent. In conjunction with the strong inflationary pressures of the period, the instability in the system no doubt affected the balance of factors considered necessary in the 1950s and 1960s to achieve economic development.

The rift between the economic development scheme and the present economic climate in Mexico is summarized by Escobedo as follows:

> In the financial sector the inflationary phenomenon has affected the savings capturing of the banking system. In real terms its internal savings decreased affecting its capacity to finance the public deficits, making it necessary to resort to primary financing from the Bank of Mexico. In order to avoid this increase in the national money supply, attempts at capturing savings at pre-1972 rates have been attempted.

But the procedure has become increasingly expensive now. The interest note differentials between the ones paid by the Mexican Banking System and the ones paid in international markets had to be greater in order to cover the exchange risk and an additional utility premium . . .; they [savings] only offer a temporal solution and therefore an unstable one.

From this exposition it is clear that in the financial sector the economic policy should not depend upon the transfers of savings that the banking system could make by means of legal adjustments, because the procedure is becoming increasingly expensive.[15]

Escobedo's comment on the present conflict between the financial community and government is interesting. It is this very partnership, developed for twenty years under the import-substitution development plan, that stimulated growth with stability. During the 1950s and 1960s, this alliance of monetary and fiscal policy reinforced the development plan. As long as the economy maintained stable growth the plan did not cause strains upon the partnership. However, the change in policies accompanying the increased federal expenditures of the 1970s created a climate where maintenance of the partnership of monetary and fiscal policy became less tenable. If this partnership is less tenable, then clearly the development plan, which Mexico chose to follow in the 1950s, becomes increasingly difficult to maintain. The cost of returning to a stable growth pattern under import substitution while maintaining present government foreign exchange objectives may not be impossible, but it will certainly be difficult. The simple monetary policies of the 1950s may not be correct options during the 1970s.

The Year 1975

Let us turn to the situation in 1975. Public expenditures (including investment) reached about 300 billion pesos, up from 216 billion pesos in 1974; the deficit increased from 64 billion pesos in 1974 to approximately 90 billion pesos, or about 10 percent of GDP. More than half of this deficit was financed by foreign borrowing, while the remainder came from domestic sources, including the Bank of Mexico. We know that the responsibility for financing the deficit was largely that of the monetary authorities, directly by money creation or through financial intermediaries. With domestic savings growth slowed, money creation became the obvious alternative. From Table 3.7 we know that domestic credit creation times its share of high-powered money ($[D/H] gD$) was 19.74 percent in 1973 and 39.30 percent in 1974. In 1975 the figure was about 50 percent. In 1975 real income growth was down to 4 percent, with inflation holding at about 15 percent. The net effect from our monetary model, once the money multiplier was considered should have been a substantial outflow of foreign reserves. Actually, there was a net inflow. The model missed by an error of more than 30 percent.

However, this discrepancy can be explained by examination of government borrowing in the fourth quarter of 1975 and the reserve balance for the fourth quarter. Almost all of the increase in foreign reserves is from fourth quarter borrowings. The underlying pressures for outflows still existed, and with this new borrowing they were exacerbated through the money supply and demand equilibrium conditions. Reserves began to leave during the first and second quarters of 1976, according to the Bank of Mexico.

With the introduction of various control programs and market barriers during the 1970s, along with export subsidies designed to maintain some parity of growth in prices of traded goods, inflation in Mexico escalated to a rate above world levels. The high inflation (more than 20 percent) of 1974 was followed by double-digit inflation again in 1975. However, by mid-1976 inflation was decelerating until the time of the currency devaluation. The wide divergence in Mexican and U.S. prices in 1974 and 1975 existed because of these barriers to price arbitrage, thereby enabling some of the excess domestic credit to be reflected in price increases rather than reserve losses. In summary, the increased deficit was due to an inelastic fiscal revenue structure inherited from the development policies of the 1950s and 1960s, combined with expansionary government expenditure and investment programs. The resulting deficit could not be wholly financed by diverting private savings to the public sector through the now less vigorous (in real terms) financial sector. Foreign borrowing was not enough to fully compensate for the deficit. Finally, the available alternative was Central Bank financing and domestic credit expansion.

The Devaluation

Upon consideration of the real growth in Mexican economic activity and U.S. price increases in 1975 and 1976, nominal money demand (in domestic money) would have been satisfied by a 12-14 percent growth (annual rate) according to monetary approach theory. Or, to state it differently, if the domestic government deficit (Y_g - t) grew at a rate such that it could be financed by borrowing from the private sector (i_b), either directly or indirectly, this would affect (Y_g -t). The remainder of the identity, new domestic credit creation, would have been sufficiently low to imply either an inflow or at least no outward pressure on reserves; that is, the domestically created money supply would have grown at a rate similar to the demand for money (between 12 and 14 percent on an annual basis).

The actual domestic credit growth rate was about 50 percent because of the sharp (almost 50 percent in 1975) growth in government expenditures (Y_g), slow growth in revenues (t), and inability of the financial sector and/or foreign borrowing, either directly or via government banks, to finance the deficit. The money multiplier offset some of the domestic factors, but domestic credit ($[D/H]gD$) growth through $Y_g > (t + i_b)$ and the money multiplier decline combined to cause a 36 percent rate of growth in domestically created money. The high growth in domestically created money was about double the rate of growth in demand for those funds. Thus, supply exceeded demand and pressures had to be relieved, according to the monetary approach, through an outflow of foreign reserves. As has been noted, forces on reserve outflow were temporarily slowed by domestic price increases and by short-term foreign borrowing that satisfied short-term money demands (although actually strengthening the underlying long-term excess supply of money, since domestic credit was still allowed to expand rapidly). These forces, according to this theory, would continue to mount until corrected by a deceleration in domestically supplied money growth equal to the growth in demand for money. If there had been no reason for reserves to flow in either direction—a flexible exchange rate—the pressure on reserves would be replaced by pressures on prices and/or the exchange rate. This is not to say that the underlying reasons that caused outward pressures on reserves were eliminated by de facto devaluation or by the October 31, 1976, float of the peso; however, these long-run pressures are now redirected. The readjustment of currencies (just as in 1954) is not in itself a cause of these forces but, more likely, a consequence.

NOTES

1. Benjamin Higgins, *Economic Development: Problems, Principles, and Policies* (New York: Norton, 1968), p. 281.

2. Arturo Ruíz Equihua and Leopoldo Solis, "Aspectos generales de los instrumentos de política monetaria y crediticia en México," unpublished working paper, Centro de Estudios Monetarios Latinamericanos, IX Reunión Operativa, Buenos Aires, November 1968.

3. Ibid., p. 24.

4. Mort Gabriel, "El banco central en el fomento de mercados financieros eficaces: Algunas experencias mexicanas," address to the Fourth Meeting of Governors of the Central Banks of the Americas, Buenos Aires, May 1967, p. 1.

5. For a more detailed study of private *financieras*, see J. A. Genel, "A Study of Some Aspects of Nonmonetary Financial Intermediation," unpublished dissertation, University of Chicago, 1973, pp. 2-17.

6. Raymond W. Goldsmith, *The Financial Experience of Mexico* (Paris: OECD, 1966), p. 21.

7. Ernesto Fernández Hurtado, "Papel actual de la política monetaria y crediticia," address to the Convención Nacional de Ejecutivos de Finanzas, Jalisco, November 2, 1972, pp. 1-2.

8. Ruíz Equihua and Solis, op. cit., p. 12.

9. Ibid., p. 17.

10. See Fernández Hurtado, op. cit., pp. 2–12; Ruíz Equihua and Solis, op. cit., pp. 17-18; and Robert L. Bennett, *The Financial Sector and Economic Development* (Baltimore: Johns Hopkins, 1965), pp. 49–54, for a discussion of the mechanism.

11. Dwight S. Brothers and Leopoldo Solis, *Mexican Financial Development* (Austin: University of Texas Press, 1966), p. 67.

12. Gilberto Escobedo, "Ahorro y desarrollo económico," unpublished working paper, 1975, pp. 12–13.

13. Ibid., p. 12.

14. Ibid., p. 14.

15. Ibid., p. 18.

As has been established, during the mid-1970s Mexico entered a period in which many of its standard economic formulas appeared to be either inappropriate or misapplied. We have seen from our analysis of the monetary approach theory the effect of a restrictive monetary policy during 1970, 1971, and early 1972—money stock actually grew as foreign reserves flowed inward. We have shown that, in 1973, the reserve growth leveled out as domestic money supply and demand were in a better balance. However, during the two and one-half years before the currency devaluation of 1976, what happened to money growth, prices, domestic credit, and foreign reserve flows? In answering this question, we first set forth the conclusions from our analysis concerning monetary and fiscal policies and their flexibility; next, we examine the implications of the policy of the mid-1970s prior to the evaluation in light of the monetary approach to the balance of payments; and, finally, we draw the implications appropriate to the de facto devaluation of September 1, 1976.

The following conclusions have been reached in this analysis. First, the notion that Mexico belongs to a unified goods, services, and assets market is true. Second, the monetary approach to the balance of payments is a useful framework for scrutinizing the effects of monetary policy in Mexico during 1954-74. Third, the Central Bank of Mexico cannot independently control the domestic money supply. Fourth, reserve flows tend to offset changes in domestically created money. Fifth, although domestic credit in Mexico is a policy variable, this study shows that the monetary authorities have less and less control over domestic credit as pressure mounts from Treasury-financed deficits through domestic credit creation. Sixth, monetary policy from 1954 through 1969 was consistent with maintenance of a balance of payments equal to or slightly greater than zero, while this was not the case for the early 1970s; that is, during the 1950s and 1960s the Central Bank expanded domestic credit at a rate similar to the rate of growth in money demand. In the 1970s the policy was alternately tight, then loose, creating shocks within the system. Finally, international reserve flows throughout 1954-74 were explained by the monetary approach to the balance of payments.

The empirical results confirm the unified market assumption with respect to prices and the interest rate. The price level in Mexico moved very closely with the price level in the United States during 1956-74. The discrepancies in 1954 and 1955 can be attributed to parity adjustment following the devaluation of the peso in 1954.

Not only was the unified goods and services market hypothesis confirmed for Mexico; the notion of a unified capital market could not be rejected. The mean growth rate of the Mexican long-term interest rate was found to be statistically the same as the mean growth rate in the long-term interest rates of Britain, Canada, France, Germany, Belgium, or the United States. Given exogeneity of prices and interest rates, the monetary approach to the balance of payments is the appropriate theory to be applied to the Mexican expansion.

Mexican international reserve flows for 1954-74 were as predicted by the monetary approach to the balance of payments. The balance of payments adjusted to the relative growth rates of money demand and domestically created stocks of money. If money demand in Mexico grew faster than the Mexican authorities wished to expand the money supply via their own resources, then reserves flowed inward. Another result was that reserves flowed in, not out, in response to an increase in real income and in the general price level, ceteris paribus. The interest rate effect on foreign reserves was weak, but conformed generally to the hypothesized negative sign.

Mexico experienced rapid growth during most of this period. Therefore, reserves generally flowed inward, despite a worsening balance of trade. The restrictive policies of deficit financing placed limits on the growth of domestic credit. The financial policies of the Central Bank, which were consistent with the general development policies, led to a stable reserve position for most of the period. A restrictive monetary policy that maintains slow growth in domestic credit, allied with rapid growth in money demand, will generate reserve inflows, regardless of the movements in the balance of trade. This is an explanation of the balance-of-payments surpluses of the 1970s. The financial authorities attempted to slow money growth by using domestic controls in 1970, 1971, and 1972; this led to the inflow of foreign reserves needed to maintain the equilibrium in the money markets.

The inelastic nature of the fiscal revenue system and the attenuated ability of the financial sector to finance government debt forced the Central Bank to play an increasing role in financing public expenditures. Alternatives open to the

Central Bank in financing government deficits were hampered by the slowdown in the growth of the financial sector and the savings rate. Increasingly, the method of financing the deficits necessarily became money creation. This effect of government deficit spending on domestic credit is confirmed empirically by the expanded model results.

Finally, the study has shown that the monetary approach to the balance of payments is a powerful tool for analyzing the relationship of monetary policy in Mexico. Throughout this period the implication of the model maintained a high degree of precision. During the early period, Mexican monetary policy was simple to exercise because the world was not experiencing rapid inflation. Monetary policy during this period was directed toward expanding the money supply at a rate commensurate with the real rate of growth. As the world entered a period of inflation during the late 1960s and early 1970s, the same monetary policy was no longer consistent with a zero balance of payments. Guidelines had to adjust to the new period. An attempt to hold to the old guidelines of slow growth in domestic money led to the foreign reserve inflows of 1970-73. It is clear from the empirical evidence that when the Central Bank attempted to administer restrictive or expansionary policies in the early 1970s, it affected the balance of payments—not the money supply.

The results are clear for 1975 and 1976. Domestic credit grew rapidly, because the fiscal deficit was financed by the monetary authorities via direct government bond purchases. The sharp increase in domestic credit creation in 1975 set in motion market mechanisms (an excess supply of money) that caused outward pressures on foreign reserves. Short-run, stopgap measures delayed the inevitable until 1976, when the pressure mounted as domestic credit was still needed to finance larger fiscal expenditures. As these pressures on reserves became apparent to the public, capital also began to leave, in expectation of imminent devaluation. Thus, the floating of the peso on September 1, 1976, was the culmination of the expansionary monetary policy of the 1970s, with the rationale for the policy directly linked to the fiscal deficit.

BIBLIOGRAPHY

BOOKS

American Economic Association. *Readings in the Theory of International Trade*. Homewood, Ill.: Richard D. Irwin, 1950.

———. *Readings in Monetary Theory*. Homewood, Ill.: Richard D. Irwin. 1961.

Banco de México. *Cincuenta años del Banco Central*. Mexico City: Banco de México, 1976.

Bennett, Robert L. *The Financial Sector and Economic Development*. Baltimore: Johns Hopkins, 1965.

Bird, Richard M., and Oliver Oldman. *Readings on Taxation in Developing Countries*. Baltimore: Johns Hopkins, 1975.

Brothers, Dwight S., and Leopoldo Solis. *Mexican Financial Development*. Austin: University of Texas Press, 1966.

Burger, Albert. *The Money Supply Process*. Belmont, Calif.: Wadsworth, 1971.

Cagan, Philip. *Determinants and Effects of Changes in the Stock of Money, 1875 1960*. New York: National Bureau of Economic Research, 1965.

Christ, Carl F. *Econometric Models and Methods*. New York: John Wiley, 1966.

Dean, Edwin, ed. *The Controversy over the Quantity Theory of Money*. Boston: D.C. Heath, 1968.

Ellsworth, Paul T. *The International Economy*. Fourth edition. Toronto: MacMillan, 1969.

Frenkel, J., and H. G. Johnson, eds. *The Monetary Approach to the Balance of Payments*. London: Allen and Unwin, 1976.

Friedman, Milton. *The Optimum Quantity of Money and Other Essays*. Chicago: Aldine, 1969.

Friedman, Milton, and Anna Schwartz, *A Monetary History of the United States, 1867-1960*. New York: National Bureau of Economic Research, 1963.

Friedman, Milton, ed. *Studies in the Quantity Theory of Money*. Chicago: University of Chicago Press, 1956.

Gensberg, Hans, *World Inflation and the Small Open Economy*. Geneva: Graduate Institute for International Studies, 1975.

Goldsmith, Raymond W. *The Financial Experience of Mexico*. Paris: OECD, 1966.

Griffiths, B. *Mexican Monetary Policy and Economic Development*. New York: Praeger, 1972.

Higgins, Benjamin. *Economic Development: Problems, Principles, and Policies*. New York: Norton, 1968.

Informe Anual 1973. Mexico City: Banco de México, 1974.

International Financial Statistics. Washington, D.C.: International Monetary Fund, various issues.

Johnson, Harry. *Further Essays in Monetary Economics*. Cambridge, Mass.: Harvard University Press, 1973.

Johnston, J. *Econometric Methods*. New York: McGraw-Hill, 1972.

Kaldor, Nicholas. *Essays on Economic Policy*. London: G. Duckworth, 1964.

Keynes, John M. *The General Theory of Employment, Interest and Money*. New York: Harcourt, Brace and World, 1936.

King, Timothy. *Industrialization and Trade Policies Since 1940: Mexico*. London: Oxford University Press, 1970.

McKinnon, R. I. *Money and Capital in Economic Development*. Washington, D.C.: Brookings Institution, 1973.

Meade, J. E. *The Balance of Payments*. London: Oxford University Press, 1951.

Meiselman, David. *Varieties of Monetary Experience*. Chicago: University of Chicago Press, 1970.

Miller, L. R., and P. Rao. *Applied Econometrics*. Belmont, Calif.: Wadsworth, 1971.

Mundell, Robert A. *International Economics*. New York: MacMillan, 1968.

Reynolds, Clark. *The Mexican Economy*. New Haven: Yale University Press, 1970.

Rutledge, John. *A Monetarist Model of Inflationary Expectations*. Lexington, Mass.: Lexington Books, 1974.

Smith, W. L., and R. L. Teigen, eds. *Readings in Money and National Income Stabilization Policy*. Homewood, Ill.: Richard D. Irwin, 1970.

Solis, Leopoldo. *La realidad económica mexicana: Retrovisión y perspectivas*. Mexico City: Siglo XXI, 1970.

Statistics on the Mexican Economy. Mexico City: Nacional Financiera, 1974.

Taussig, F. W. *International Trade*. New York: MacMillan, 1927.

Theil, Henri. *Principles of Econometrics*. New York: John Wiley, 1976.

Thorn, Richard S., ed. *Monetary Theory and Policy*. New York: Random House, 1966.

Viner, Jacob. *Studies in the Theory of International Trade*. New York: Harper, 1937.

Wilford, W. T., and R. Moncarz. *Essays in Latin American Economic Issues*. New Orleans: Division of Business and Economic Research, Louisiana State University, 1970.

Williamson, Jeffery G. *American Growth and the Balance of Payments 1820-1913*. Chapel Hill, N.C.: University of North Carolina Press, 1964.

Zahn, Frank. *Macroeconomic Theory and Policy*. New York: Prentice-Hall, 1975.

ARTICLES

Aghevli, Bijan B., and Moshin S. Khan. "The Monetary Approach to the Balance of Payments Determination: An Empirical Test." Paper presented at American Economic Association convention, San Francisco, December 1974.

Borts, G. H., and J. A. Hanson. "The Monetary Approach to the Balance of Payments." Unpublished working paper, Brown University, 1975.

Brunner, Karl, and A. H. Meltzer. "Predicting Velocity: Implications for Theory and Policy." *Journal of Finance* 18 (May 1963): 319-54.

———. "Some Further Investigations of Demand and Supply Functions of Money." *Journal of Finance* 19 (May 1964): 240-83.

———. "Comment on the Long Run and Short Run Demand for Money." *Journal of Political Economy* 76 (November 1969): 1234-40.

———. "Money Supply Process and Monetary Policy in an Open Economy." in *International Trade and Money*, ed. M. B. Connelly and A. K. Swoboda. London: Allen and Unwin, 1973.

Chenery, Hollis, and W. Bruno. "Development Alternatives in an Open Economy: The Case of Israel." *Quarterly Journal of Economics* 76 (September 1972).

Chow, Gregory C. "On the Long Run and Short Run Demand for Money." *Journal of Political Economy* 74 (April 1966): 111-31.

Cox, W. Michael. "Rational Expectations, the Monetary Approach to the Balance of Payments, and the Role of Monetary Policy in the Open Economy." Unpublished working paper, 1976.

Cox, W. Michael, and D. Sykes Wilford. "The Monetary Approach to the Balance of Payments and World Monetary Equilibrium." Manuscript, 1977.

Díaz-Alejandro, C. F. "On the Import Intensity of Import Substitution." *Kyklos* 18 (1965): 495-511.

Dornbusch, Rudiger. "Expectations and Exchange Rate Dynamics." *Journal of Political Economy* 84, no. 6 (December 1976): 1161-76.

Eckhaus, Richard S. "Estructura del sector de las financieras en México, 1940-1970." *CEMLA boletín mensuel* 21 (May 1975): 156-287.

Escobedo, Gilberto. "Mexican Stabilization Policy, Fiscal or Monetary?" Unpublished working paper, 1973.

———. "The Response of the Mexican Economy to Policy Action." *Federal Reserve Bank of St. Louis Review* 55 (June 1973): 15-23.

———. "Los indicadores para medir el resultado de la política monetaria en México." *Comercio exterior* 23 (October 1973): 1007-15.

———. "Ahorro y desarrollo económico." Unpublished working paper, 1975.

Fernández Hurtado, Ernesto. "Papel actual de la política monetaria y crediticia." Address to Convención Nacional de Ejecutivos de Finanzas, Jalisco, November 2, 1972.

Frenkel, J. "A Monetary Approach to the Exchange Rate." *Scandinavian Journal of Economics* 78 (May 1976): 200-61.

Friedman, Milton. "The Demand for Money: Some Theoretical and Empirical Results." *Journal of Political Economy* 67 (August 1959): 327-51.

———. "Interest Rates and the Demand for Money." *Journal of Law and Economics* 9 (October 1966): 71-85.

Gabriel, Mort. "El banco central en el fomento de mercados financieros eficaces: Algunas experiencias mexicanas." Address to Fourth Meeting of Governors of the Central Banks of the Americas, May 1967.

Gómez Oliver, Antonio. "La política monetaria y el nivel de precios en México." Working paper, Centro de Estudios Monetarios Latinamericanos, 1974.

———. "La demanda de dinero en México." In *Banco de México, Cincuenta Años del Banco Central.* Mexico City: Banco de México, 1976.

Groves, H. M., and C. H. Kahn. "The Stability of State and Local Tax Yields." *American Economic Review* 40 (March 1952): 87-102.

Hume, David. "Of the Balance of Trade." In his *Essays, Moral, Political and Literary*, I. London: Longmans Green, 1898; reprinted in *International Trade Theory. Hume to Ohlin.* New York: W. R. Allen, 1965.

Johnson, Harry G. "The Monetary Approach to the Balance of Payments Theory: A Diagrammatic Analysis." *The Manchester School* (1975).

Kemp, Donald S. "A Monetary View of Balance of Payments." *Federal Reserve Bank of St. Louis Review* 57, no. 4 (April, 1975): 14-22.

King, David T. "Purchasing Power Parity and Exchange Rate Flexibility: 1973-1975." *Southern Economic Journal* 43, no. 4 (April 1977): 1582-87.

Komiya, R. "Economic Growth and the Balance of Payments." *Journal of Political Economy* 77, no. 1 (January-February 1969): 34-48.

Laffer, A. B. "Monetary Policy and the Balance of Payments." *Journal of Money, Credit, and Banking* 4 (February 1972): 13-22.

Laidler, David. "Some Evidence on the Demand for Money." *Journal of Political Economy* 74 (February 1966): 55-68.

Lebon, Jules. "The Real and Nominal Effects of Devaluation: The Relative Price Effects of Exchange Rate Changes." (Unpublished.)

Legler, J. P., and P. Shapiro. "The Responsiveness of State Tax Revenue to Economic Growth." *National Tax Journal* 20 (1968): 46-56.

McClure, C. H., Jr., "The Proper Use of Indirect Taxation in Latin America." *Public Finance/Finances Publiques* 30, no. 1 (1975): 20-45.

Magee, S. "Empirical Evidence on the Monetary Approach to the Balance of Payments and Exchange Rates." *American Economic Review* 66 (May 1976): 163-70.

Meltzer, Allan H. "The Demand for Money: The Evidence from the Time Series." *Journal of Political Economy* 71 (June 1963): 219-46.

Monte Mayor, A. "La demanda de dinero: El caso de México." Unpublished thesis, Faculty of Economics, University of Nuevo Leon, 1969.

Mussa, Michael. "A Monetary Approach to the Balance of Payments Analysis." *Journal of Money, Credit, and Banking* (August 1974).

Porter, M. G. "The Interdependence of Monetary Policy and Capital Flows in Australia." *Economic Record* 24 (August 1974): 120-50.

Porter, M. G., and R. J. Kouri. "International Capital Flows and Portfolio Equilibrium." *Journal of Political Economy* 82 (August 1974).

Putnam, Bluford. "International Price and Interest Rate Differentials and the Monetary Approach to the Balance of Payments." (Unpublished.)

———. "Non-Traded Goods and the Monetary Approach to the Balance of Payments." Paper presented to the Eastern Economic Association, New Orleans, April 1976.

Ruíz Equihua, Arturo, and Leopoldo Solis. "Aspectos generales de los instrumentos de política monetaria y crediticia en México." Unpublished working paper, Centro de Estudios Monetarios Latinamericanos, IX Reunión Operativa, Buenos Aires, November 1968.

Rutledge, John. "Balance of Payments and Money Demand." Paper presented at Southern Economic Association meetings, New Orleans, November 1975.

Tanner, J. E., and V. Bonomo. "Gold, Capital Flows, and Long Swings in American Business Activity." *Journal of Political Economy* 76, no. 1 (January-February 1968).

Thompson, John K. "Financial Markets Development as a Technique for Achieving Non-Inflationary Growth: Mexico, 1954-65." Manuscript, Federal Reserve Bank of New York, 1976.

Wilford, D. S. "The Demand for Foreign Reserves in Mexico." Unpublished Master's thesis, Vanderbilt University, 1973.

———. "The Velocity of Money and Financial Development in Mexico." Manuscript, Federal Reserve Bank of New York, 1977.

———. "Price Levels, Interest Rate, Open Economies, and a Fixed Exchange Rate: The Mexican Case, 1954-1974." *Review of Business and Economic Research* 12, no. 3 (Spring 1977).

Wilford, D. S., and W. T. Wilford. "The Revenue-Income Elasticity Coefficient: Performance and Stability Criteria." *Public Finance* 31, no. 1 (1976): 103-15.

———. "The Revenue-Income Elasticity Coefficient: Performance and Stability Criteria." *Review of Business and Economic Research* 12, no. 2 (Winter 1976): 90-93.

———. "Monetary Approach to Balance of Payments: On World Prices and the Reserve Flow Equation." *Weltwirtschaftliches Archiv* no. 1 (1977): 31-39.

———. "A Note on the Monetary Approach to the Balance of Payments: The Small, Open Economy." *Journal of Finance* (forthcoming).

———. "On Revenue Performance and Revenue-Income Stability in the Third World." *Economic Development and Cultural Change* (forthcoming).

Wilford, W. T. "State Tax Stability Criteria and the Revenue-Income Elasticity Coefficient Reconsidered." *National Tax Journal* 17 (September 1965): 304-12.

———. "Comment on Stability, Growth, and the Stabilizing Influence of State Taxes." *National Tax Journal* 28, no. 4 (December 1975): 452-59.

Wilford, W. T., and J. M. Villaususo. "Central America: The Demand for Money in the Common Market." *Economic and Social Studies* 24, no. 2 (June 1975).

Williams, W. V., R. M. Anderson, D. O. Froehle, and K. L. Lamb. "The Stability, Growth, and Stabilizing Influence of State Taxes." *National Tax Journal* 26 (1974): 267-74.

Zecher, J. Richard. "Monetary Equilibrium and International Reserve Flows in Australia." *Journal of Finance* 29 (December 1974): 1323-30.

Zecher, J. Richard, C. Burrows, and L. McGregor. "Determinants of the Australian Money Supply Since 1950." Paper presented at Congress of Australian and New Zealand Association for the Advancement of Science, August 1972.

D. SYKES WILFORD is an economist at The Chase Manhattan Bank. He has been a faculty member of the University of New Orleans, economist for the Federal Reserve Bank of New York, and a consultant to various agencies. In particular, he was consultant to the United States Agency for International Development/El Salvador in 1975.

Wilford has published a number of articles in professional journals that deal with the monetary approach to the balance of payments and fiscal revenue structures. In particular, articles appearing in *Weltwirtshaftliches Archiv* and *Public Finance* deal with Mexico.

Wilford earned his B.S. degree from the University of Tennessee, his M.A. degree from Vanderbilt University, and his Ph.D. degree from Tulane University.

DEPENDENT INDUSTRIALIZATION IN LATIN AMERICA:
The Automotive Industry in Argentina, Chile, and
Mexico
Rhys Owen Jenkins

ECONOMIC NATIONALISM IN LATIN AMERICA:
The Quest for Economic Independence
Shoshana Baron Tancer

FINANCING URBAN AND RURAL DEVELOPMENT THROUGH
BETTERMENT LEVIES: The Latin American Experience
Jorge Macon
José Marino Manon

THE USE OF INDEXATION IN DEVELOPING COUNTRIES
G. Donald Jud